Grass

ROBERT GRAY

Grass Script

Selected Earlier Poems

CARCANET

First published in Great Britain in 2001 by
Carcanet Press Limited
4th Floor, Conavon Court
12–16 Blackfriars Street
Manchester M3 5BQ

Copyright © Robert Gray 2001

The right of Robert Gray to be identified
as the author of this work has been asserted by him in accordance
with the Copyright, Designs and Patents Act of 1988
All rights reserved

A CIP catalogue record for this book
is available from the British Library

ISBN 1 85754 511 7

The publisher acknowledges financial assistance
from the Arts Council of England

Set in Monotype Garamond by XL Publishing Services, Tiverton
Printed and bound in England by SRP Ltd, Exeter

Contents

from *Creekwater Journal* (1974)
- Journey: The North Coast — 7
- The Farm Woman Speaks — 8
- The Thief — 9
- Morning — 10
- Nine Poems — 11
- Back There — 12
- On Climbing the Stone Gate Peak — 13
- Within the Traveller's Eye — 14
- The Pine — 16
- A Labourer — 17
- 'The Single Principle of Forms' — 17
- Eleven Poems — 18
- The Meatworks — 19
- To the Master, Dōgen Zenji — 21
- Bright Day — 24
- Ten Poems — 25
- The Sawmill Shacks — 26
- North Coast Town — 31

from *Grass Script* (1978)
- Late Ferry — 33
- Poem to Kristina — 34
- In the Bus — 36
- The Chair — 37
- Old House — 39
- Pumpkins — 40
- 'The old wooden venetian blinds …' — 41
- The Visit — 41
- Flames and Dangling Wire — 42
- Eight Poems — 44
- Dharma Vehicle — 45
- Telling the Beads — 59
- 'Smoke of logs …' — 61
- Brushtail Possum — 61
- Going Back, on a Hot Night — 62
- Twelve Poems — 63
- Reflection — 65
- Scotland, Visitation — 65
- The Dusk — 67

from *The Skylight* (1983)
    Dark Glasses   69
    'In the early hours ...'   70
    Motel Room   71
    On Contradictions   71
    Travels *en Famille*   73
    Smoke   74
    The Canoe   75
    The Sea-Shell   80
    'The best place ...'   81
    Bondi   82
    Sketch of the Harbour   84
    Emptying the Desk   85
    Ten Poems   86
    A Day at Bellingen   88
    Landscape   89
    Bringing the Cattle   90
    Karl Marx   91
    Watching by the Harbour   92
    Diptych   93
    Aubade   96
    Memories of the Coast   97
    For Harriet   100
    At the Inlet   100
    Mr Nelson   102
    Curriculum Vitae   106

from *Piano* (1988)
    Black Landscape   111
    A Port of Europe   112
    Very Early   114
    Rainy Windows   115
    Byron Bay: Winter   116
    A Garden Shed   117
    Harbour Dusk   120
    Eight Poems after Kusadao   120
    Plurality   123
    Walking Around at Night   126
    Prunus Nigra   128
    Fire Sermon   128
    Other People   129
    Sixteen Poems from the Japanese   130
    The Shark   133
    Description of a Walk   136
    A Winter Morning   137
    A Summer Evening   138
    Nine Bowls of Water   139

Creekwater Journal (1974)

Journey: The North Coast

Next thing, I wake up in a swaying bunk,
as though on board a clipper
lying in the sea,
and it's the train, that booms and cracks,
it tears the wind the apart.
Now the man's gone
who had the bunk below me. I swing out,
cover his bed and rattle up the sash –
there's sunlight rotating
off the drab carpet. And the water sways
solidly in its silver basin, so cold
it joins together through my hand.
I see from where I'm bent
one of those bright crockery days
that belong to so much I remember.
The train's shadow, like a bird's,
flees on the blue and silver paddocks,
over fences that look split from stone,
and banks of fern,
a red clay bank, full of roots,
over a dark creek, with logs and leaves suspended,
and blackened tree trunks.
Down these slopes move, as a nude descends a staircase,
slender white gum trees,
and now the country bursts open on the sea –
across a calico beach, unfurling;
strewn with flakes of light
that make the whole compartment whirl.
Shuttering shadows. I rise into the mirror
rested. I can leave my hair
ruffled a bit that way – fold the pyjamas,

stow the book and wash bag. Everything done,
press down the latches into the case,
that for twelve months I've watched standing out
of a morning, above the wardrobe
in a furnished room.

The Farm Woman Speaks

Winter has arrived, the winds scour this place.
Feeding the children broth,
I show them now, through the dull windows,
trees rocked with a cruel cough.

We can't take a bad year,
but the lino looks like an over-ripe banana –
there's no help pacing the floors.
Leaves panic with claws on the verandah

from trees that boom all day. Usually
you don't notice the noise until night,
but if you wake then, you'd swear the sea had come
crashing inland; that awful fright

passes as you realize
where you really are, and where we are
is with crops burnt by frost, the cows
eating dry cornstalks, with all of our care

about three children and the little money
sunken here; with the pasture grass
of a morning, in this worst season for years,
thick with crushed glass – .

Of a morning, I see him let the gates fall open.
The moon thaws. Wind floats bubbles
out of a magpie – and bears upon a salver
the croak of the crows.

He jerks in boots toward the shed,
buckets pulling at his neck.
A fig tree is clenched on the earth, and strain bulges
its tendons. The fences slop either side, gone slack.

Three are still the times when he will turn to me.
At night, I drowse by the persimmons in the log,
and, first, he puts an arm around me – .
Only, those flames then feel like a striding flag.

The Thief

Not the man who was dying for so short a time, and for such
an economic return,
and not as urgently the one there waiting
resurrection, but the other man
with these, who was simply dying – it is this one,
the pouted body
silk-white for a moment in the late afternoon,
stands above us,
while ever we feel as if there were only Jesus
splayed, in mockery of flying,
on the shaven wood.
It was not three but thousands
braced on those nails,
becoming rigid with agony, and lava-streaked with blood.
Speak of one other
under the leaping whips;
who was pegged there, his head wobbling like a top petering out;
the hair, dredged weeds;
flies in the nostrils, and strung blood in the mouth;
warped in that shape
above the city,
until there were only birds upon his bones.
We save no feeling for this pain.
On the day, people came to look,
and the guards could go through with their hammering;
they helped each other
emblazon the thief. And for an endless time

he must have known
how the sunlight slid thickly as oil amid the olive boughs,
and men reached out for wine and bread,
and dew came in the leaves
the way that stars appear. His own weight was sealing up
his lungs like
mucous lips.
People disregard this still, who never seek
in their prayers or belief
some expiation. We are only concerned
with Jesus, who is like all gods
for our gain.
Natural, no doubt, but not an end, since Jesus would use and
    condemn
a Judas, as part of His scheme. All of that
is the hollowest metaphysics we have dreamed; and all
of the thief's sufferings
are ours alone.

Morning

    Feeding chickens, pollard scattered like wet sand.

    They jump down stolidly from their roosts
    as an old sailor jumps
    with wooden leg;
    in there, underneath half a corrugated-iron tank,
    open-ended.

    I'm stepping around the bare black ground;
    wire-netting propped
    on lopped poles.
    Moss about, bits
    of brick poking through, and bones.
    Rusted wrench
    pressed into the round, jaws open –
    a tyrannosaurus head. Reeds.

In packing cases, one side gone, the eggs
in dry grass.
On this cold morning, they're warm, smooth:
Surprising stone

almost weightless.
Bent over;
at the side of my face, the silver
liquid paddocks, and steam.
My eyes and nose are damp, I see through my own smoke.

Finding the eggs, dry – the colour of dry sand.

Nine Poems

In the rock pool, grass
moves with the water. Violin bows
adagio.

At dusk, scything
under trees by the front gate;
pale moths rise.

The back fence caught
in a wave by Hokusai –
the morning glory vine.

These ripe days,
the heat, the tenderness;
a white bathtub filled with green water,
leaves against the glass.

A few cars, way off
on the freeway, over wide fields –
a lost burst of tracer fire
through the bright afternoon.

On this peak, alone,
it feels as if my shirt
is trying to go back.

Sultry night, fast clouds.
The moon's an aspirin
dropped in water.

Chopping wood,
I strike about at mosquitoes
with the axe.

Smokestack, evening sky;
the smoke, a woman's long hair,
hung underwater.

Back There

A farmer, in brittle morning,
struggles with the solid milk cans, his gasping
all around him –

Across the yard
of scarred
mud, the tangled branches
iron lace,
and a shed is going down sideways
under convolvulus.

There's moss
on the walls
one side of the house.
A rusty plough
is stranded like the horns of a
twisted neck,
out in the mouldy
grass.

And over the raw, stripped paddocks, up
on
the windy skyline,
children run,
capering
all about that huge nerve-end,
a bare tree;
flickering, black.

On Climbing the Stone Gate Peak

(As if by a poet of the T'ang Dynasty)

In a floating gown, I have come among these promontories alone;
the path is struggling on like a wounded snake.
The crags above Stone Gate are piled one upon the other:
it seems as if they will topple from out of the rushing mist.
All about on ledges cling the twisted pines;
all over the rocks there is moss, like a discoloured snow.
I wander into a dark copse, which the late sun pierces,
and in this gloom, a pool of scarlet water.
The haunts of ape and deer have been left behind;
only a bird now cries out mournfully, in search of its mate.
I climb by caves where dripping water rings like crystal,
and leaves of dwarf bamboo are dripping –
it is because of a waterfall thrown down, beyond here, on stones;
the splintering of a white jade staff.
That long pole of water goes on being shattered,
yet is no more diminished than Liu-hai with age.
Across the vibrating pool, a light smoke is windborne,

and drifts above me, the spirit of a great bird.
I climb again, breaking the cobwebs of mist;
vines are trailing from the cliffs beneath which I find my way.
Then, coming from a crevasse, gaze on other mountains.
They are blue and green inks, that are rolled upon slanted silk.
How could one live among such pinnacles, but with the True Mind,
which asks for nothing, but is open to all that is?
These rugged peaks will not prolong one gentle configuration,
and yet I find here strange flowers (that are struck like an instrument).
Only one who knows Detachment, and lets his thoughts grow
   fleeting,
could love these mountains, since his mind is not hampered
   anywhere.

Within the Traveller's Eye

A late afternoon. From this passing train
one sees the forest.
It is like a cupboard, in some deserted room,
with its door ajar.

There has been rain. Now, so late, the sunlight reappears.
We are flying low, through these small country towns....

Morning glory vines grow over the wire fences
in the shape of huge snowdrifts.
Someone fat is leaning heavily on his verandah rail.

And the old pine trees in a loose main street,
where sparrows live like fleas.

We go above the mud and fallen light of an estuary;
a few birds rise.
The river, towards evening, is moving slowly
under a slow sky.

Seeing these small towns, there returns to mind
the life of a tired woman —

It is those lavatories, out in the back yards
overgrown with paspalum;
the wet cardboard box, lying about;

the piles of weathered palings stacked on trestles;
a floor-cloth, that the dog has taken.

It seems there was always this shallow afternoon light.

Steep iron roofs, old wooden places;
they face each other in gravel side streets,
with rainwater ditches out of which the grass stands,
a ramp across to each.

There is a utility moving
behind tall roadside heads of grass,

a child's white apron.

A man is walking on the long shadows
of the telegraph poles, going for cigarettes and matches
to the shop.

I know those dim, unused sitting rooms:
faint gleam of lino
among the rugs, and everything in there as rounded
as Melba's bodice.
The fringes on everything.

All through such a house was the smell of boiled vegetables,
and of something else
living amidst that odour –

it was the sexual rancour, stored away
like china or cuff links,
and never spoken.
There only the second-best was ever used.

As daylight is turned low
in the grass, people by the kitchen windows,
or in the outside bathroom, at the end of a verandah,
can hear again the frogs

and crickets
begin, out in those flat, soggy paddocks.

But we have gone now miles beyond a town.
The shadow of the tallest mountain
in the valley wall

is lengthening over an empty plain of grass
we move across.

And it feels
this shadow is going to indicate, as though it were a finger,
a grave, lying open
somewhere here.

And you have to try to turn your face away.

The Pine

With a snow-cap
only
of needles;
aslant. And the lopped-off
branches of
various lengths
about its trunk.
The rhythm amongst these
such
a music, all
by chance.
Alone
in the back paddock
in the yellow grass.

A Labourer

He goes out early, before work, half asleep,
webs of frost on the grass; wading
paspalum to the wood-heap,
a bone-smooth axe handle pointing at him. It lifts the block
on a corner of beetled, black
earth. The logs are like rolled roasts,
they tear apart on red-fibred meat. The axe squeaks out.
Lifting it –
the head pulls backwards –
now he sinks to where he is. And the new tile roofs
encroaching about
in the thin water of the sun;
the lavatories towards here, up the back yards.
Roosters scream
through iron, spurred timber
left stand. Bringing the axe down
bounces gong-blows off the ground, raises the crows;
forging off with rusted cries
into the steam. He takes an armful of the kindling
to drop in the box beside the stove,
and splinters hang
from a red, hieroglyphed hand –
These for the child, who's father to the man;
sitting-up, so reluctantly,
in the small mist of his breakfast.

'The Single Principle of Forms'

All day a storm has fermented. Now the clouds are huge above the mountains.

A horse stands in the paddock and swings its wooden face at the flies.

It stands with one hind-leg poised lightly by the other, like the way a male ballet dancer stands.

The muzzle is soggy as the stump of a freshly-cut banana palm.

And that coarse long tail makes you think of an Indian, waiting
with a tomahawk amongst the forest.
    The horse trembles its flank in the heat, and now lightning
shudders –
    A silverish lightning, over those great haunches of cloud.

Eleven Poems

Sanding the floorboards;
across the house, in a blank window,
hibiscus flowers.

On the enamel dish, slice open
a pear.
Rain hangs in the window gauze.

Soaking in the hot bath;
on a radio somewhere
the time-pips. Three o'clock.

I get up. It's bright
moonlight. The sea is a glass brimming
under the tap.

Some children's voices,
a piano, in the hollow School of Arts.
In the alley, rain floats.

Long wet verandah,
leaves blown in. Where could our souls live
but on the Earth?

Hot night. In the yard,
tightening the tap. It still drips.
The mosquitoes come.

Passing on a train;
sheets borne out from a clothes-line
and the pasture-land.

Huge, glittering stars.
Looking up, out among the frogs
croaking, croaking.

The new moon —
fallen out of its gown,
a white breast.

A drop hung
indoors, from the tap's blunt
beak. A bird sings.

The Meatworks

Most of them worked around the slaughtering
out the back, where concrete gutters
crawled off
heavily, and the hot, fertilizer-thick,
sticky stench of blood
sent flies mad,
but I settled for one of the lowest-paid jobs, making mince
right the furthest end from those bellowing,
sloppy yards. Outside, the pigs' fear
made them mount one another
at the last minute. I stood all day
by a shaking metal box
that had a chute in, and a spout,
snatching steaks from a bin they kept refilling
pushing them through
arm-thick corkscrews, grinding around inside it, meat or not —
chomping, bloody mouth —
using a greasy stick
shaped into a penis.
When I grabbed it the first time
it slipped, slippery as soap, out of my hand,
in the machine
that gnawed it hysterically a few moments
louder and louder, then, shuddering, stopped;
fused every light in the shop.

Too soon to sack me –
it was the first thing I'd done.
For a while, I had to lug gutted pigs
white as swedes
and with straight stick tails
to the ice rooms, hang them by the hooves
on hooks – their dripping
solidified like candle-wax – or pack a long intestine
with sausage meat.
We got meat to take home –
bags of blood;
red plastic with the fat showing through.
We'd wash, then
out on the blue metal
towards town; but after sticking your hands all day
in snail-sheened flesh,
you found, around the nails, there was still blood.
I usually didn't take the meat.
I'd walk home on
the shiny, white-bruising beach, in mauve light,
past the town.
The beach, and those startling, storm-cloud mountains, high
beyond the furthest fibro houses, I'd come
to be with. (The only work
was at this Works.) – My wife
carried her sandals, in the sand and beach grass,
to meet me. I'd scoop up shell-grit
and scrub my hands,
treading about
through the icy ledges of the surf
as she came along. We said that working with meat was like
burning-off the live bush
and fertilizing with rottenness,
for this frail green money.
There was a flaw to the analogy
you felt, but one
I didn't look at, then –
the way those pigs stuck there, clinging onto each other.

To the Master Dōgen Zenji
(AD 1200–1253)

Dōgen came in and sat on the wood platform;
all the people were gathered
like birds upon the lake.

After years, home from China,
and he had brought no scriptures; he showed them
empty hands.

This in Kyoto,
at someone-else's temple. He said, All that's important
is the ordinary things.

Making a fire
to boil the bathwater, pounding rice, pulling weeds
and knocking dirt from their roots,

or pouring tea – those blown scarves,
a moment, more beautiful than the drapery
in paintings by a master.

'It is this world
of the *dharmas* (the momentary particles)
that is the Diamond.'

•

Dōgen received, they say, his first insight
from the old cook of some monastery
in China,

who was on the jetty
where they docked, who had come down
to buy mushrooms

among the rolled-up
straw sails, the fishnets, brocade litters,
and geese in baskets.

High sea-going junk,
shuffling and dipping
like an official.

Dōgen could see
an empty shoreline, the pinewood plank of the beach,
the mountains

far off
and dusty. Standing about
with his new smooth skull.

The horses' lumpy hooves clumped on those planks,
they arched their necks
and dipped their heads like swans,

manes blown about
like white threads from off
the falling breakers;

holding up their hooves as though they were tender,
the sea grabbing at
the timber below.

And the two Buddhists in all the shuffle got to bow.
The old man told him, Up there,
that place –

The monastery a cliff-face
in one of the shadowy hills.
My study is cooking;

no, not devotion. No,
no, not your sacred books (meaning Buddhism). And Dōgen,
irate –

he must have thought
who is this old prick, so ignorant
of the Law,

and it must have shown.
Son, I regret
that you haven't caught on

to where it is one discovers
the Original Nature
of the mind and things.

•

Dōgen said, Ideas
from reading, from people, from a personal bias,
toss them all out –

'discolourations'.
You shall only discover by looking in
this momentary mind.

And said, 'The Soto school
isn't one
of the entities in Buddhism –

don't even use such names.'
The world's an incessant transformation, and to meditate
is awareness, with no

clinging to,
no working on, the mind.
It is a floating; ever-moving; 'marvellous emptiness'.

Only absorption in such a practice will release us
from the accidents, and appetites,
of life.

And upon this leaf one shall cross over
the stormy sea,
among the dragon-like waves.

Bright Day

The fantail is tying
loosely
a complex knot,
as if as an illustration,
about one spot
in the air

and then drawing it sharp;
yanked-tight
noose
on some frailer string –
the tangled line
in the sun
of a beetle, or other living thing;

throttling it.
It chops that end
short, and
this fantail, in its mantilla –
the swirling,
the blur –
goes off once more, taut;
not far

Again,
like some applause-igniting
artistry,
it flourishes a
variation
on that elaborate bow –
is adding, everywhere,
its satin
finishing touches to the morning.

Ten Poems

I'm getting up later –
these stormy nights of autumn.
Sailboats on the lake.

4 a.m.; the Milky Way
blown high over the forest.
A truck changes down.

So hot, the sparrow looks ill,
sitting on the tap handle.

Lean in the wash-up,
trying a poem. On the dark,
scratches of rain.

Weary, I tear open the shopping.
From newspaper waddles
like an irate duck
this melon.

The pleasure of weeds:
to see them beneath the street-lights.

The train's halted
nowhere. Small birds whirling about
through the weeds.

Drunk last night, waking
with limbs scattered on the bed.
The shiny leaves move.

Lunchtimes, the ball
smokes about dry grass. Tall chimneys
trail their smoke one way.

In the dim foyer
these calico-coloured flowers
that keep on hoping.

The Sawmill Shacks

The shacks are overgrown on the mountainside
we come rattling around
in Ted's bomb. A dirt road,
metal clang
under the car; the trail
to a waterfall.
Silent, chill
bush below,
the tree-tops tattered,
smoke-blue; high,
shot-to-pieces shapes against a frail
wintry sky. Halfway
on the cold
volcano, as steep
as sawdust
under a chute, once, in this dead
(oil-dirt and rusty cog)
crawled-through town.
At the top of the dry creek-bed of the street,
a furnace: rusted
cone with a round
tip, its sieve-like
smoke vent. An old Chev
timber truck's sunk
like a bullock down, almost gone,
blind.
The stores and shacks
are shingled weatherboard,
lines scored,
their boards curling
away. Huge ferns
spout through the boardwalks and
fungus is spreading everywhere, like bright
dried apricot.

Just out, above the road,
the Community Hall,
weathered salmon-pink, slipping
through weeds, some planks held by

one nail.
Inside,
a boarded-up gloom, dust
in the door-beam
on the breathless floor,
furry.
A hollowness,
splattered with bird-lime. There's
a book on the floor, flaked
to rusty shale –
Baroness Orczy,
'property of
the C.W.A.' And a Sunday school print
on the wall: a saint bestowing
rhetorical blessing,
smouldering, through the nicotine-coloured
stain.
A piano, with the seeming grin
of old bones:
caries, and the teeth's
enamel gone....

You hear the rudimentary violin;
stamping boots
and a sudden dog-like yelp; tea cups scrape;
the whining, dogmatic women's voices,
and their squawks;
a bellowing, out of florid jowls; those songs
of places they could hardly imagine:
Sacramento,
no doubt, and San Antonio,
and one would have been Phoenix....

Gladys, Clarrie, Madge and Arthur:
concerned about
the hint
of a slight;
with this mind, that is too often like

a knocked-over
hive.
So little to do, anywhere here,
but resume;
their lives become a long time.
Women who'd cry

without finding any tears,
who startled themselves, wondering where this was;
those men
who did not pause at twilight,
whose solution was to put on
a snarl;
people the same as any —
blown away
out of a stony, slanted gap.

They have got lost again, somewhere.
On the mouth
a taste of pity, thinking of us.
The rafters are clotted with nests
and, treading about,
from inside the piano
a dead-animal stench. You have to push out,
under cobwebs
(the door-screech), stepping
jerkily in thin sun. And a crow lurches away
slides down
far off
we soar
over the vague blue mountainside....
How the tree-tops there
like wave crests
glint
in the last, reaching,
spatulate beams. And this huge dome

of air:
navy-blue, porous; the
blue of endless-
ness.
Inside your chest, you feel yourself arising. —
Other mountains

far along from here, like skyscrapers
at dusk
with all of their lights out,
in the faint mist.
This opened-up
melon, of the evening.

Out here,
the long grasses
are swirled
loosely
like a buoy.
And now the stars,
the first few,
clear
as water
on a grass blade,
appearing,
effortless
as stars appear....

But we catch ourselves standing about. – It is
a sound of water
underneath the groaning of this
tethered avalanche –
the piled-up
heights of the forest –
everywhere.
And all that trickling water
seems an evil sound, in such a place:
speaks of
black, icy leaf-mulch
that it sinks through; and of spreading over bald, slimy ground;
of the roots
standing out, furry, from frozen soil
like rib-cages;
a
deranged scrawl
of sharp-toothed lantana,
where only it can pass –
in the enormous day-long gloom
behind those torrential lines
of forest.

As if for a ballet,
all the light has fallen out of the sky,
and cold rears up,
the wind rises from the left.
Hard to see
the timber-getters' shacks,
each as lightless and empty,
as cast-off,
as a skull, staved-in.
This cold!
It reveals to you, like a disease, the shape of your bones.
Stumble down,
and now the headlights are swung solidly about
on a dank
cellar of leeches. —
Feeling our way
through all four wheels of the car
out
into the long valley. And
dropping here

easily as an owl glides,
across these paddocks upholstered in powdery weeds. —
The moon's
now fully risen,
afloat
in an immense fine spray
like perfume,
filling all the valley.
And one already said of nature
it is not 'human-hearted'; except that, in men it is,
in some men.
Whatever is added to nature
nature's made.
Dimly you feel
out of what endless dissatisfactions
we have come.

North Coast Town

Out beside the highway, first thing in the morning,
nothing much in my pockets but sand
from the beach. A Shell station (with their Men's locked),
a closed hamburger stand.

I washed at a tap down beside the changing sheds,
stepping about on mud. Through the wall
smell of the vandals' lavatory,
and an automatic chill flushing in the urinal.

Eat a floury apple, and stand about. At this kerb
sand crawls by, and palm fronds here
scrape dryly. Car after car now – it's like a boxer
warming-up with the heavy bag, spitting air.

A car slows and I chase it. Two hoods
going shooting. Tattoos and greasy fifties pompadour.
Rev in High Street, drop their first can.
Plastic pennants on the distilled morning, everywhere;

a dog trotting, and someone hoses down a pavement;
our image flaps in shop fronts; smoking on
past the pink 'Tropicana' motel (stucco, with sea shells);
the RSL, like a fancy-dress Inca; the 'Coronation',

a warehouse picture show. We pass
bulldozed acres. The place is becoming chrome,
tile-facing, and plate-glass; they're making California.
Pass an Abo, not attempting to hitch, outside town.

Grass Script (1978)

Late Ferry

The wooden ferry is leaving now;
I stay to watch
from the balcony, as it goes up onto
a huge dark harbour,

out beyond that vacant, thin jetty;
and palm tree tops
make a sound like touches
of the brush on a snare drum

in the windy night. Going beyond
street lights' fluorescence
over the dark water, a ceaseless
activity of chromosomes

uniting and dividing; and out beyond
the tomato stake patch
of the yachts, strung with their orange
glow; leaving this tuberous

small bay, for the city
across an empty dark. There, neon
redness trembles down in the water
as if into ice, and

the longer white lights
feel nervously about in the blackness,
towards here, like hands
after the light switch.

The ferry wades now into the broad
open harbour, to be lost soon
amongst a silver blizzard of light
underneath the Bridge:

a Busby Berkeley spectacular
with thousands in frenzied, far-off
choreography, in their silver lamé,
the Bridge like a giant prop.

This does seem in a movie theatre:
the boat is small as a moth
wandering through the projector's beam,
seeing it float beneath the city.

I'll lose sight of the ferry soon –
I find it on darkness,
and savour it like honeycomb,
filled as it is with its yellow light.

Poem to Kristina

I
I remember a time, on sandy wheel tracks,
amongst all that sharp hot machinery, the bush –
Your flouncing, tired walk;
coming back, feet puffing up the dust,
carrying your sandals;
petulant, grizzling, and laughing with me about it,
but still close to anger,
and knowing that I knew.
I can see myself trying to be humorous for you.

2
Amongst the rocks, I broke open
and persuaded you about your first oyster,
also. Talking like a cage full of birds, and
posing, gesturing, like a samurai,
to get your courage, you swallowed it
and with a scream leapt up
onto the sudden bracket of my arms,
and clung there wriggling your legs, and squealing,
and laughing out something. You liked it.

3
Your face, so often, ready to take offence;
defensive, hurt, if my eyes flickered
away while you talked all your unsure rush of talk.
Or you presented it with those hours of
barely any make-up. Posing, as playful and artificial
as photos of Marilyn. And I,
your human 'mirror
mirror on the wall' – a responsive mirror
of flesh, for you to confirm, with my startled look,
what you found in the glass one.

4
At night, you wouldn't use the outdoor lavatory
last thing, for fear of spiders. And for fear
of the dark, you made me come outside
so you could pee. You bared your cream cheese
behind, beneath the clothes-line, and would remark
about all the tree of stars,
with your brown thighs splayed apart, like Havana cigars.

5
On grey days, out the kitchen window,
we watched the grey water moving by in the lake –
a crowd through turnstiles. Mooching about,
listening to our few records over and over;
in the half-light of the house, their combed Valentino sheen.
Making sandwiches at the sink, and putting on,
after enquiry, the Tim Buckley, or an Otis Redding, or Van
    Morrison.
And sitting there, leaned together,
like two horses out in the yard in the rain.

6
Now I sit and look back. And we write sometimes;
we keep in touch, as they say.
I remember those times when I was happy
and didn't think I was. Strange, the way
only now I recognize it
as happiness. That that should be what happiness is like.
Too late, as people say.
It's true. The worst is, you begin to suspect
there's to be realized, in life,
a homily as often
as we did not believe.

In the Bus

In the back of an old country bus, down a bitumen side road through the floating rain. All the school kids dropped off, we're going on to the next town; and now you can hear the frying-pan splutter underneath and the flap of wipers.

On a rattling wood bridge we slow to look at the yellow creek rising; water coming over some usually dry large stones, where there's foam like a curtain-end beating out of a window. And through a paper mill forest – here every pine, I realize, will have this shredded lank grey water all over it, delicately as pollen upon a stamen.

Going on, to the shouted speculations of a couple of women, a farm worker and the driver; the puddles in the aisle throwing a straight punch on the corners; the steamy smell of wet wool. The rubbed-off windows are again grey, and on their outside is pebbled water, that trembles like the face of a honeycomb covered with bees.

Although, there is the teeming green of the bush wherever a trickle of water has seeped in and is moving down the glass like some small water-tufted animal that goes slowly along out there oblivious, keeping its head down all about the ground in the rain.

The Chair

Sitting out
a chair in the garden
morning sun
fine gravel among
outbreaks of flowering bush
ferns
a twisted surging white
log
lain in the open
the waterlily
stepping stones

Roof cracking in the heat
bird claws
all over it
this one-time farmhouse
a stain
like a grazed shinbone
on its long slide
tin

I see the grey-brown
fine bowled-over grass
in flat paddocks
fences
stitching it all
corroded smoky line of the bush
one coil
of the scaly river

And have to go back in
too hot
the chair's left standing
out
in the blazing yard
wooden
looming
in the sun

I can see it through these glass doors
in moving about
the hot shadowy house
getting up to spray flies
or to get a drink
the chair is standing its ground

And I want to sleep
I would like to be a seed
deep in the earth
I want
a dream of water
lying
in the mouth
a creek that rises
into a cave under the bank
and to wake at nightfall
when the autumn is already coming on
leaves falling

The chair will be standing outside still
the fallen leaves
upon it
it is like a working-man
bringing for me the basket
in his arms

Old House

In the long, windy grass
on the headland,
against a deep sea,
the closed wooden house, with its verandahs
and observatory.

The roller blinds are drawn;
a late sun throws
the shadow
of railing and bars, onto the weatherboards,
askew.

All that grass is rippling, the way hounds
undulate
on the scent. Out to sea
only the cold hoofprints of the light
are left. A white yacht.

The yacht appeared from amongst
the wrung grass
of the slope,
silently,
and is folded back now, along the coast.

The crack of its going-about,
and the cry
of a gull, echoed
in the bare verandah.
Down an institution's corridor, a white coat.

Pumpkins

What in novels is called 'a grizzled stubble'
on these pumpkin leaves.
The leaves shuffle
as you wade amongst them, their bristles
rustling.
One is slowly stepping upon
egg shells,
pagodas of orange peel,
on heaps of tea slops.
And the pumpkin flower,
a big loud daffodil.
You push about darkness, parting the leaves.
A rooster is on this slope, also;
come to peck
outside, in the late afternoon.
It is putting down its spur
with care,
and its eye is flickering about.
The rooster is red
and lacquered as a Chinese box;
a golden hood
down to its shoulders, like a calyx, flexible
upon its body, as it pecks,
flicks,
flicks, and blinks,
pecks. I'm holding one foot up, looking for
somewhere
amongst this vine. And find
the pumpkin –
segmented like a peeled mandarin
or leather
on the back seat of a thirties tourer.
I break the stem
and lift the heavy, warped pumpkin,
just when the vine's become
too dark.
In between pink and yellow,
its orange tone
can be added easily to the sunset
that's been going on.

I take the pumpkin beneath my arm.
Like a bad painting, this magnificent sunset.

'The old wooden venetian blinds ...'

The old wooden venetian blinds are closed. I put my case down and open them with an arm that I can hardly raise. The backyard's a scrawl of paspalum; just large enough for a rusted rotary clothes hoist.

    The striations of light coming into the room are like the city's escalators in rows, with the dust drifting along them....

The Visit

Blown onto the coast road, I go to see my mother,
unexpectedly.

I walk down the same dirt country street
with duffel bag,

and find her in the garden; her prolapsed belly.
She is grey – so grey.

Her hands, lined with the garden dirt,
fly to her face, and hair.

Straight away, she must think of something to eat.
On back steps, wintry sunlight gossip.

I play some old records. Where I left has grown over.
My brother comes for lunch

and on the quiet he tells me she is not so good.
She does become tired suddenly,

'because of the shock', and has to rest.
I wake her last thing,

late in the afternoon. I must be in Brisbane tomorrow;
must catch the bus. Her soft loose skin.

But I'll write. She says that she won't worry
now she's seen me. Reaching up.

I go out, to grab a book I remember I have left here,
find her sleeping again.

Flames and Dangling Wire

On a highway over the marshland.
Off to one side, the smoke of different fires in a row,
like fingers spread and dragged to smudge.
It is the always-burning dump.

Behind us, the city
driven like stakes into the earth.
A waterbird lifts above this swamp
as a turtle moves on the Galapagos shore.

We turn off down a gravel road,
approaching the dump. All the air wobbles
in some cheap mirror.
There is a fog over the hot sun.

Now the distant buildings are stencilled in the smoke.
And we come to a landscape of tin cans,
of cars like skulls,
that is rolling in its sand dune shapes.

Amongst these vast grey plastic sheets of heat,
shadowy figures
who seem engaged in identifying the dead –
they are the attendants, in overalls and goggles,

forking over rubbish on the dampened fires.
A sour smoke
is hauled out everywhere,
thin, like rope. And there are others moving – scavengers.

As in hell the devils
might poke about through our souls, after scraps
of appetite
with which to stimulate themselves,

so these figures
seem to be wandering despondently with an eternity
where they could find
some peculiar sensation.

We get out and move about also.
The smell is huge,
blasting the mouth dry:
the tons of rotten newspaper, and great cuds of cloth....

And standing where I see the mirage of the city
I realize I am in the future.
This is how it shall be after men have gone.
It will be made of things that worked.

A labourer hoists an unidentifiable mulch
on his fork, throws it in the flame:
something flaps
like the rag held up in 'The Raft of the Medusa'.

We approach another, through the smoke,
and for a moment he seems that demon with the long barge pole.
It is a man, wiping his eyes.
Someone who worked here would have to weep,

and so we speak. The rims beneath his eyes are wet
as an oyster, and red.
Knowing all that he does about us,
how can he avoid a hatred of men?

Going on, I notice an old radio, that spills
its dangling wire –
and I realize that somewhere the voices it received
are still travelling,

skidding away, riddled, around the arc of the universe;
and with them, the horse-laughs, and the Chopin
which was the sound of the curtains lifting,
one time, to a coast of light.

Eight Poems

White rowboat,
slowest wingbeat. A hotel window's
flower-patterned air.

Cold afternoon fields;
the lights of a roadside shop
fill the puddles.

Racing to the surf,
they strike its silver, crooked
as roots of ginger.

Coming down, through dusk –
white flowers scattered in the bush
the milking-shed lights.

Drying her eyes,
outside on the hilltop street;
hiding in the wind.

A cafeteria
with few there. All the table-tops
in wide morning light.

The city across the harbour,
or stumps of a gully
in the smoky morning bush.

The torch beam
I feel with, through the pouring night,
is smoke.

Dharma Vehicle

I
Out of the reach of voices
in the wind.

Camping at a fibro shack
fishermen use –
swept with tea-tree branches, and washed down
with kerosene tins of
tank water.

Like banners raised,
all these eucalyptus saplings –
the straight trees.

A sea-breeze
over the grass headland, where fallen, white
branches swim;
leaves here
are shaken all the time,
shoes that run
on stone.

My bed
a pile of cut fern.

•

And the Pacific Ocean mornings
in windows rinsed with
wet handkerchief,
among the whitish-grey, ragged paperbarks –

that glint
all over,
in long shoals,
of translucent
scales.

At night,
lying by the fire
outdoors – seeming to lean above
moon and stars afloat.

The distant cannon
of the waves....

The paperbarks climb
slowly,
and are spreading out, like incense-smoke.

•

I read beneath the trees all day,
caught-up
with those old Chinese
who sought the right way to live, and found
one must adapt to nature,
to what is
outside our egotism;
who loved this earth.

'Here I am
gulping the stuff from the fountain
and willing to let it
trickle out of my mouth.'   (Lucretius)

In India, the Buddhists
praised insensibility
to the world
('Doth not the Hindoo
lust after vacuity?');
but with Buddhism's arrival in China,
by the T"ang,
in the time of Hui-neng, the sixth
patriarch, there'd come
a complete reversal of such *dharma* –

There is the Other Shore,
it is here.

•

It is not reaching into any deep centre,
but to awaken the mind without fixing it anywhere.

A man who goes into trance
and has no thought or feeling   (Hui-neng)
surely is no better than a block of stone
or bit of wood.

But to know pleasure as pleasure
and pain as pain
and to keep the mind free from all attachment
is what's called No-Thought.

•

I turn out the lamp.
Leaves, twigs, berries falling
on the tin like rain
in the night.
– It was the monk
Fa Ch'an-ang, in China,
dying,
heard a squirrel screech
out on the moon-wet tiles, and who told them
'It's only this.'

•

Only this.
A wide flat banana leaf,
wet green,
unbroken, leaning on
the glass.

The mother-of-pearl of a cloudy dawn.

2

How shall one continue
to confront every morning
this same face in the mirror?

Anxiously peering,
demanding –
such intolerable self-pity;

hysterical, and without decency.
Impossible marriage
with such a face, that eats up other people.

I do not want to be this sort of cripple
in the world any longer;
not for any of my excuses for being

to remain,
not for any of my possibilities.
I do not want to be what I am.

I'm woken here,
I would like simply to walk away.
And live without saying that I live,

without me
as the filament, the grains, the sedimentary content,
the matter to be taken into account.

And continue,
but without this continuing; certainly,
not to remain defender of such a proposition,

which, every next moment, life is going to contradict,
and with the back of its hand,
and with its fist.

•

When you are suffering
and you want to be free
of that which torments you,

it is not greed,
is it?
This is something more basic than

the calculations of thought.
And this is why I've felt
it's possible

to elude the mind,
whose confusion has continued
for too long.

The summer's almost gone.

3
The holymen whom Gautama sought-out in the forest –
torment of a leper –
knew about Transience,
as did Heraclitus, about this time,
but taught there is a soul,
Atman,
'I',
and that it's the same as the World-Soul, Brahman,
of abiding nature.
Gautama saw there is no cure for the Self
in such belief.

'I saw the thorn
that is piercing to the heart of men' –
and belief in the soul is part of its poison –
the thorn
is one's subjective desire,
to which a man clings above all,
tenacious like the shark
and as cruel –
'If this thorn is drawn out
one is calm and knows peace.'

He could not find his relief among those *sannyasin*,
and so, went on alone;
staring in
where all the other's knees had failed them –

on the edge of the buffalo pasture
in blue smoke of moonlight,
in the wet grass,

with mud running on his body;
or among tree roots,
and there he saw the ragged wild flight
of the stars,
a particular night –
it was like,
as many others have said, since then,
'the bottom falling out
of the washtub',
or
'like flowers suddenly blooming
on withered trees'.

•

'No God, no soul' –
It is all like a mountain river,
travelling very far, and very swiftly;
not for a moment does it cease to flow.
One thing disappears and determines what is arising,
and there is no unchanging substance
through all of this,
nothing to call permanent,
only Change.
That which is the substance of things
abides as nothing
and has nowhere
a nature of its own.
Its essential nature is Nothingness.

•

In Western thought, this recalls something that Engels said
in 'Dialectics of Nature' –
that 'motion is the mode of existence
of matter';
there is no form of matter that isn't in transformation
and therefore
no form that's an essence.

'Matter, as such,'
Engels wrote, 'is the pure creation of thought ...
an abstraction';
matter only exists in particular forms.

So that these transient things, themselves, are what is Absolute;
these things
beneath the hand, and before the eye –
the wattle
lying on the wooden trestle,
pencils, some crockery,
books and papers, a river stone,
the dead flies and cobwebs
in the rusty gauze.

4
I am woken here when 'the sun gets to its feet
shouting'.
The sun takes a stride,
'wearing its waistband of human hair'.
I go out, over the morning's copious small water,
never touched,
and the golden breath covers the dense forest and the mountains,
the paddocks below
that are streaked with dead trees.

I walk down a long slope
where the bush is cut far back on either side;
the early sky, so light,
has a feeling of
the first day up again after illness;
the dew is dashed in the grass,
blue,
gold, red; as you pass above,
it lights up, everywhere you walk.

From this hillside
I can see, beyond a solid, wind-levelled, slant mass of trees,
the ocean –
like silver foil
that's been crumpled and smoothed again.

And below me, dark timber,
with those topmost cauliflower-clumps of eucalyptus
scattered, opaque,
against the ocean light.
Inland, there are banana plantations
right along, over the billowing hillslopes,
and a few tin roofs
lit-up like dangling water-drops.
I hear, faintly, a dog yap,
and can see blue smoke
that is staggering along the air a little way.

I go further down;
wade a lagoon of whisky-coloured grass
onto the dirt road (soaked
to the knees), and pass
a deserted schoolhouse, with its red iron roof and tank,
and tennis court
lying within wire netting; and now a flock
of parakeets
sweeps by – it banks
on the morning, dark lift of wings – is settling
everywhere.
They're leaping about amongst the trees, and some dip into the
    court,
vague behind wire
as if flying through mist –
wheel up again
catching the sun – their feathers then
the colours of that dew....

5
It was in China that men first could say
of this transitory world
it is Nirvana.

The Taoists had seen the universe is Self-Existent,
and that all particular things
spontaneously arise.

'If Heaven had produced its creatures on purpose
it would have taught them to love (Wang Ch'ung)
and not to prey upon each other.

Rather, all things have come about through Transformation,
because they are one.
You do not find anything superior to things.'

Such a universe was spoken of as a Great Furnace
in which all that is
shall burn.

It is a fire that consumes the fire, undiminished.
How could Heaven have pity for that fate
its nature brings about?

'Though all is in destruction and regeneration at once
there is tranquillity in this disturbance. (Chuang-tzu)
Tranquillity in disturbance is called Perfection.

There are ten thousand things being transformed,
and the sage is transformed along with them
without difference, without end.

Therefore, his movements are effortless as water;
his stillness, deep like a mirror;
his response, an echo.

His rarefied condition makes him seem to disappear.
He accepts his body with pleasure,
forgetting life and death.

To him there is nothing in the world that is greater
than the tip of a hair
that grows in spring.'

•

When something comes into existence
it is because of conditions that are favouring –

all-that-is, being interdependent,
combines to bring it forth,

and thus nature is good to man,
or at least, it's more favourable than against him.

And everything appears, the Taoists said,
in dialectical relation –

it is like two stags
that lock horns close to the ground – a sound

of bamboos knocking together –
whose playful blood grows erect

in their veins: pushing
they manoeuvre

and stagger,
the dust arises

as all of these floating worlds.
On each world

and in every event of each
the same two stags contest.

And Lao-tzu, on leaving the Empire of Han,
at some vast age, to die –

riding on his buffalo
that was like a torrential rain –

wrote a poem to the people, and left it with the border guard:
that men should confess

it is the opposite of what we love
is good to us,

that it's only this weeping
which can make us glad.

•

The things of the earth
fill men with life
and swarm, like red corpuscles to a wound,
to do them good.
The earth feeds men aright;
the five grains are to feed them,
and the beans,
and the leaves for their soup;
and the water for the same,
it goes down alive
inside men; and these fruits,
they feed men well.
And even Death –
the vinegar
that is found in the dish.
One ought to go out
into the forest and sun,
bathe in the streams and ocean,
and care for the body with oils
and comb the hair and decorate oneself
to sleep with another,
and join one's friends
in the grove of summer,
or beneath wide eaves
in dark weather, when the rain drips,
bringing wine.
And wander along the mountainside alone.
Because life is fleeting,
it is the breath of a bull in the wintry dusk.
Throwing away the self, 'let us hasten
to enjoy this life'.

6
The image of Buddha became a fat Chinaman
who was rolling on his haunches in a fallen-down robe,
twiddling as a fan
the end of a banana leaf,
with tits that wouldn't have looked out of place on a sow
and a laugh like a slice of watermelon –
to tear-up the conceptions of the mind.

Onto that way in harmony with nature there was joined
the sharp means of Release.
Before this, the Taoists were content with passivity,
and for discarding the self, most often
made do with wine.
The Emperor Wu-ti was first to hear the Unique Insight,
who asked of Bodhidharma
define Buddhism.
Bodhidharma replied: Vast Emptiness.

•

Ma-chu got up onto the wood platform,
eased his legs in the Lotus,
laid aside his fan;
he started to trail smoking water on the green tea powder,
beating it with a whisk,
and looked over wet gravel, the heads of all the assembly,
between the darkness of wide, heavy doors,
to a lemon colour in the garden;
then he said to them, 'There is no Buddhahood for you to attain;
cling to nothing, that is the Tao',
and signalled for the crack
of the woodblocks together, for them to leave;
and sipped from the bowl, alone.

•

And there was a Master, Hsuan-chien,
told his students, after they'd sat in the courtyard for many days,
prostrating themselves, to be taken in,
'Pull on your clothes of a morning
and work along the hillside with the others,
or rake the leaves,
until you hear the dinner drum;
eat your meals,
and go to the john when you have to –
That's all.
There's no transmigration for you to fear, no
Nirvana to achieve.
Just respond to all things
without getting caught –

Don't even hold on to your Non-Seeking as right.
There is no other wisdom to attain.'

•

An afternoon rain
is drifting like sails of smoke
among these paperbark trees, about the shack;
it is the crumpling sound of cleaning up
cellophane wrap, close by,
and in one place, the green slap
of cow water.
'Sit straight, in Padmāsana, like a mountain,
keeping count of the breath, over and over,
so as not to touch your thought,
the eyes left open.'
You cannot dwell anywhere.
Realizing, beyond the intellect, that 'I' do not exist.

There is a soft, wet, vivid green,
a paddock, that rises
full as a breaker's first lifting,
now, after the cold steam;
and above it, struck by watery sun,
scaffolding tree-trunks, branch-beams, obliques, that shine
whitely, out of the black cumulus of bush.
And I hear rain tapping,
as if on canvas, from the guttering, and from where
a bird has skittered
all about this window, shaking the wet tree.

'A mind that's like a mirror,
in which things pass and leave no stain.'

7
I'm coming back with a haversack from the shop,
a beach resort
miles off,
walking all the way at the water's edge
along the empty sand.

Those shops they have forgot
to wind.

The one street, an old faded print,
squints in the glare;
outshone
by the plate-glass sea.

And I climb, one after the other, over
the headlands, on rock,
in late afternoon,

looking out to where all the clambering, wilted,
flaring

Ocean

begins, of a sudden, its bellowing and stamping,
the lowering of its shoulders,
a smoke-spray
blowing from them.

The surf comes in as though alive and tearing free
from under a net of foam –
making its break
with the panicky, bounding gallop of some great animal up
hopeless
onto the slippery shore.

And all the time along the horizon
those clouds,
that are like mountains with cliffs and valleys, now,
in the last, stretched-out sun –
that dreaming, far-off,
impossible land.

Night comes
quickly, over the water, as if water
flowing into the space left by the withdrawing sun,
and foam spreads
flatly all around me, phosphorescent,
bubbling and crackling in crab-holes in the sand.

The waves flicker
like a book left in some vast, empty house,
to a noise of doors slamming.

I am weary and cold, by now.
No one about.
Only, across the rising moon's long beam,
a bird flies,
skimming the horns of the sea.

This long beach,
beneath the immense imagery of night
and the night-bird's croak,
keeps on disappearing into the mist and dark.

And at such times, 'even in the mind of the Enlightened
there arises sorrow',
so it's all right.

Telling the Beads

One drop is laid in each nasturtium leaf,
round as mercury,

and there are several on
every looped frond of the long flat grass;

these
clear sacs of plastic, tucked and full.

Plump, uncontained water,
precipitous,

held together by the air.
They are the most fragile particulars.

On grass that's loping everywhere,
in all the trajectories of a flea circus.

Thought balloons,
you infer

that I should fill each of you with its
apt word

which must be of a like transparency.
You are the mushrooms

conceived on the pure walls of the air;
anti-pebbles;

doodlings of a Botticellian elegance.
O claritas,

one thinks of lenses, floating upon each other,
dreamed by Spinoza

before a window full of sky,
all the Christians out of the house and gone to church.

You are the digits of nature's prodigality.
You slip

on these stalks
as though one had become aware of the film

on strained eyes.
Presented on a febrifugal greenness –

someone who hadn't realized a need for refreshment
is made aware of an unventilated taste.

Looked at,
you offer hardly more than that.

This is authentic manna, it contains
no message and no promise,

only a momentary sustenance.
Run the drops from a stalk across your lip

they're lost
in the known juice of yourself, after the ungraspable

instant. Long-reputed but unresponsive
elixir.

Experiencing you, I see before me all the most refined
consolations of belief and thought.

'Smoke of logs ...'

Smoke of logs and drifting rain out in the paddocks. Those rolling paddocks are long grey waves, far at sea, beneath the blowing rain. And the dark line of bush, a crowd of emigrants at the rail.

Brushtail Possum

Thumps the water-tank
from out of the Gothic winter persimmon tree,
ticks like the start of rain
on tin
of the verandah
as we sit about after tea.

The banana leaves are shredded
like buckskin,
sway in night wind
against a closed window,
the fuel stove crackles,
the lamp-light an oily yellow.

We take some bread out:
a possum hung
over the sag of the guttering,
blackish-grey,
short-eared, snouted, anxious stare,
it swipes the bread with a human claw.

Eats it there;
nose pink and wet as a tongue,
tightly-packed fur
like moss. One eye is blue-white,
blind
from a twig or fight.

The whiskers wide-spread like a spider's web.
The face twitching about
looks down
with its live eye
as with the one that's matching the moon,
against a salted sky.

Going Back, on a Hot Night

Now we are coming again towards a station;
out of the dark
countryside, the lights of a town,
beyond these sandy flats with their paperbark.

Over a hollow long metal bridge rumbles
the long train,
like a consignment of metal beer barrels
tumbled on concrete. And I see the small moon

above a dark sea, with the moonlight
in saucers, stacked-up,
teetering. Glimpsed as it reaches out
to mark the horizon. Now we almost stop;

creak forward. Street-light, palings. Archerville.
I know the Mail –
that I can stretch my legs a while
past these sacks and hampers, along the gravel.

I see a tea-leaf scrub, and the low moon again,
procession of one;
yellow kitchens; smoke; the pond-life of stars.
Through wide paddocks dart, like mice, a few cars.

I stand about. The frogs' hollow, ringing, regular
'clonk, clonk', from the scrub –
exactly the sound of a distant hammer
on framework. Going after some labouring job.

Twelve Poems

Waking at a station,
across the blue-lit glass
this cold, far galaxy,
the rain.

A flag luxuriates:
the gestures of someone
taking a hot bath.

Rowing, linen tide,
bronze, shadows, ibis, farm lights,
linen shadows, glide.

In a dark room
rustle of the long clothing
of the rain.

Across the level
eucalypt forest, the sunlit
afternoon sea.

Signal box, somewhere;
the railway crossing sundown,
and windy dunes. ...

Small hotel, morning rain.
Reading in bed
by a soapy yellow light.

Alone, eating watermelon;
a back porch.
Seeds taken from
the lips, like hair.

Wild, dark sea, and rain
falling. Through the lighthouse beam
a great bird flies.

Struggle to cut
a slice – now the pumpkin brays
like a mule.

Hot wind,
long boards of the verandah;
a bare rope clothesline
fluttering its hairs.

A long twilight,
milky-grey. Raindrops on the window,
gulls on the grass.

Reflection

Evenings, there are people with no intention of buying
who stop to look through the fish shop glass –
men with noses that are soaked full of alcohol,
old women who speak to the hand-led children that pass.

Water runs down these windows in clam-shell pattern.
Within, there's bounty, stainless fittings, clean light,
heaped prawns, and flounder white as ice cream,
the lairs' highway, the suburbs in their mangrove night.

Scotland, Visitation

North of Glasgow, the train wound like a kite's tail,
in the first spring weather,
under the clambering, close horizon –
the skyline, semaphore.
And the brown grass, at that time, with such perfected
bright enamel
for a sky, reminding us of Australia,
of deeply-rolling, open country out from Kyogle;
except for the crooked
Japanese-scrawled, blackened pine trees,
instead of sparse eucalypts,
and the sudden tambourine-jangle of light through the beech leaves.
It is a landscape of great beauty, with small visual tradition –
yet the Flemish blue of the lochs, like the Virgin's robe,
and the upturned hillsides
piebald in broken snow,
that was brilliant like a tropical sand.
Below those hills there were stiff, damp shadows,
pastel rocks, purplish-grey,
the red cattle that are like flood-wrack
hanging near stranded water,
and the bulging long slopes, bound down in stone walls like string.
We passed the upholstered sheep-lawns
reaching to a lawn-like sea,

and grey gables sleeping before a page of the Sound.
And then, neat English cars on the turf,
and the white lacquer and old stone of our ventilated sea town.
Like Richard Hannay,
we colonials were spoiled, for the spoiled southern home-country,
and had fled north. I walked all day
on the moor, alone,
with some genetic string plucked and vibrating within.
The only other moving thing,
except for a few sheep, that barely moved,
was the shadow of a bird, hung
different places on the grass –
although, in that bright sunlight, I could not find it above.
And just at dusk, there was a lone white bird, hurrying
in the distance
along dark water,
before the corroded façade of a pine forest,
so I turned back.
A blade at my face, now.
The black promontories, spiked and furry with trees,
drifted in the misty loch.
And it was then that I could see, beyond them, in the furthest
    uplands,
dark, brutal-shouldered forms
amongst a cauldron-smoke....
And I thought there of how, like children, men have done that
which is done to them. The apparent spirits
in the earth have taught us. Our fear
and humiliation bred hatred.
And yet the earth is Empty. It is innocent.
As everything, I realized, of that replete ground's cruel history,
was, in a last consideration, innocent.

The Dusk

A kangaroo is standing up, and dwindling like a plant
with a single bud.
Fur combed into a crest
along the inside length of its body,
a bow-wave
under slanted light, out in the harbour.

And its fine unlined face is held on the cool air;
a face in which you feel
the small thrust-forward teeth lying in the lower jaw,
grass-stained and sharp.

Standing beyond a wire fence, in weeds,
against the bush that is like a wandering smoke.

Mushroom-coloured,
and its white chest, the underside of a growing mushroom,
in the last daylight.

The tail is trailing heavily as a lizard lying concealed.

It turns its head like a mannequin
toward the fibro shack,
and holds the forepaws
as though offering to have them bound.

An old man pauses on a dirt path in his vegetable garden,
where a cabbage moth puppet-leaps and jiggles wildly
in the cooling sunbeams,
the bucket still swinging in his hand.

And the kangaroo settles down, pronged,
then lifts itself
carefully, like a package passed over from both arms –

The now curved-up tail is rocking gently counterweight behind
as it flits hunched
amongst the stumps and scrub, into the dusk.

The Skylight (1983)

Dark Glasses

They lend a camera-lens intensity, and isolation,
in the sun-bathing heat,
to the blue hydrangeas across the lawn, whose each perfect dome
is made up
of unwavering jabs of mauve; and to a chipped laminate
cane stool, in between, that stands
palpable to sight
on the pencil-shaving grass.
The fence is coated with a small-leafed, dripping vine
like wallpaper:
each curlicue's edge
that sharply drawn. I turn my sight
on the equally sharp
definition of these potato chips scraps of bark
lifted on the grass,
above the tilt and scrabble
of ants, and feel myself trickle in the slowly
tightening press of the sun;
playing a breath-constricting, dangerous game.
The cicadas dilate and contract
as one, like fingers screeching down
plastic walls, in
crazy, rhythmic monotony. The sky
is an injection of maximum
blue, straight into the soul.
Supine, I prise myself up a little off the towel, to look
where she's standing at the hose,
beneath the verandah,
in the bottom of her bikini, drinking
and spraying at her daughter

behind the windows. She comes back cripple-
footed on the grass,
laughing and awry, so that water shakes either way
from her loose breasts, still white.
— I rotate my head down, a
few ratchets,
quickly, to see, above the dark glasses,
her breasts,
that are white as ice-cream
in her tan:
oiled and wet,
they look as though in syrup, or honey; each decorated
with a quince-coloured fruit.
And they feel,
I'd say, rather like
very fine, damp plastic bags do, when tightly packed with honey.

'In the early hours ...'

In the early hours, I have come out to lean in the empty corridor of the train, as it's crashing and lurching through the night.

A liquified dark scrub. And those paddocks where silverish-grey mist is rising, slowly as a stirrred moon dust.

The orange moon, like a basketball fumbled on waste ground, is bouncing across the tops of the dark forest.

In the frosty, thick night a single farmhouse light floats wetly as a flare.

I have lain awake in such a bed, and it has seemed to me, also, it would be sufficient to be one of those carried within this wind-borne sound....

(And I can remember, too, the mail train: a fine chain of lights as I stood in the paddocks of a wintry dusk. Its sound was that of wind through the swamp oaks.)

Motel Room

You keep on thinking of someone who woke here in the night,
lying still partly clothed amongst this bed,
when the television screen was a small animal, bundled-up,
shrill and squirming,
within a soiled white sheet;
and of how his mouth felt like a public place –
the phlegm, fumes and scraps
on the pavement of his tongue.
He couldn't remember which motel he was in –
the Sapphire, Blue Pacific, Palm Terrace, or Shangri-la.
The semi-trailers were meat-grinding
outside on the highway, as now;
getting down into the gristle and the bone
just here. He lifted himself, to wallow after the lavatory,
clothes twisted all over him,
and noticed how the things that he'd dropped everywhere
didn't change the look of no one's place.
He made it back, onto the bed. Near this red lampshade
whisky left in its bottle
would have looked like petrol. And he raised his head,
again, to feel about
through the coverlet, and to sniff at this chewing-gum
wad of pillow – and fell back,
relieved if he could remember
at least there hadn't been a girl in here, that night.

On Contradictions

The black swan drifting
suggests a cartoon
about a Victorian lady,

who is all refinement and propriety with
a bustle.
But on land

it's at once a lurching
tough — the whole body
like shoulders;

it doubles
and then stretches-out, flexes,
a threatening

length of neck;
the mussel-shell beak clacks
and drips;

a leathery
slap on the stones,
and hissing.

Then it leaves
along the water, and once more
is calm

as a paddle-
wheeler, on some idle
pleasure course.

There's a sublime
duplicity. It is the *belle epoque*
and the boiler room.

With millinery's most extravagant
bouquet —
the tail-feathers,

that are each curled inwards
fluffily
from the sides.

And these live feathers have all
the ashen colour,
the tremor, and frailty,

of the layers of a newspaper
burning
in a daylight clear flame.

Travels en Famille

She began at once to use the train compartment
as though it were a room at home –
we'd arrived in our hammered, canine furs,
along the platform, through the rain,

and she hung the child's bright socks,
our overcoats and scarves on anything
that seemed a hook. With her best smile
which stayed there, like a transfer.

Two old women, under rugs, were cackling
their uncertainty. The man was cornered
behind a newspaper like a dented visor.
She dried the child's feet on her tartan skirt.

How 'embarrassing'. – I could peel open a book,
as usual. Schoolgirls were grinning through
a glass partition over the women's heads;
they tried their winking on me, and then wrote

something in fog along windows of the corridor
to squeal about, and at once rub off
for one another, aghast. The train jerked
as if given a great kick, and started running

almost at once above an open countryside.
A photograph of assorted river gravel
montaged on one of sodden, moss-bright fields.
Everything creaked like a soldier's gaiters.

The electric light, warm butter; and our coats
stirring thickly around in their steam.
She read out the child's story, and we all laughed.
Besides us, a wall in two equal shades –

the dim green earth and a mauve-grey sky.
A few trees at the fields' edge, as on a shelf,
like old pieces of steel *art nouveau*; their foliage
the shapes of Japanese fans. I thought

A perfect moment, but then forgot about it.
We came to a small, flat town lying in the rain
and through its empty streets a sunset light appeared
shining on the sides of wet wooden houses.

Smoke

As if through a slanted blind,
the sun is made shafts among the immense rungs
of a Moreton Bay fig –
it comes sliding between that Gaudi-like, visceral architecture;
a slow,
egg-thickened, steamy
mixture, precisely-sliced and,
in rows, gently conveyor-belted down.
I watch across a road of
cattle-race traffic, and above the wall.

Over there, a gardener is at work:
his leaf-smoke
only visible within the slatted sun.
Discontinuously, smoke rises
and rears back, slides downward along itself, and winds
about, is gathered-up again, swelling into vast Chinese dragon
    sinuosities.
And, calmly, it seems giving birth; it keeps wavering and shredding,
then remerging, within the one great shape, like Taoist water
    symbology –
above all the interpenetrating, harsh lunging past here.

I'm waiting around beside a shopwindow's deep pool;
looking in sideways, I watch the people –
the threshings and winnowings of the city –
come right up and pass me blindly; leading with their faces
into their lives.
By turning to either side, I see
in the panels of sunlight across the way, or in this glass,
either the eternal process, as it has been stylised and revealed,
or its particulars,
that are like smoke.

The Canoe

a pod
for the hand

is the canoe in
the mind

like a hammock
this dialectic

of the soporific
and cautious

it is tandem skiing
but we

are launched
trees

fallen in the river
steep

from the bank
steeping

the dawn's
grey weather

in the black boughs
bits

of pink and lemon
brightening

like watered
sherbet

the tide
is tightly stretched

a first
sunlit passage

the bees
of day

the curled leaves
are carried

high
and lightly

processional
into deep shade

from silence
the whip bird's

long
smoothly-peeled

call
that breaks off

wetly
a green

overhang
and the high-lifted

twigs
and dust

membranous
water

now the river's
a sunlit

empty plaza
on the far shore

the tree-line
is burned away

by glare
a forest highway

and we
lone refugees

with
a perambulator

cobalt sky
the bush

like overgrown weeds
tall banks

of orange clay
a folded

duck's body
gliding

duck-breasted
swivel

these mountain slopes
built

of stacked-up
tree clumps

dead trees
scratched

down the forest's face
in a smoky dark

glassiness
and the river drops

downhill of a sudden
takes

rotored flight
straps tight

the chest
a wild bumping

aeroplane
but with lots of

shoving off
off

off
we try

and then running out on
roller-skates

to
come creeping through

the sleeping
dark

under cliffs
in the crow-calling

silence
of late afternoon

a grey
marshland

where the river gives
itself away

before the high
long silver

of the sea
and the backyards

along these slopes
with wash

flying
a rusted chassis on

a mud bank
the mangroves

collapsed
footballers' scrum

in blue mud
then

caravan parks dogs
kids yelling

we land at
the estuary

a small town's
marina

and walk through
summer dust

paddocks
above the sea

into town
to a restaurant table

in the dusk
watching

the lights of the ships
going by

The Sea-Shell

White as crockery,
it stands on the ledge of the long verandah window
in a white plank wall.

The trellis-lights –
negative, scrap shapes – are swung in here stiffly
as torch beams.

The shell is a lifting spinnaker.
And close-up, there are patterns in beige,
similar to a feather's.

The shell is wound
the same as pastry, and it has the same decorative
ruffled edging.

Coloured lead inserts in these bare windows.
Vine-patterns are stirring. Conifers,
bird movements. A Sunday.

The sound in the shell
is that of the whole Order at their evening meal,
along dim passages, behind doors.

The shell is cool, remote;
its shape causes a peristalsis in your palm,
it is breast-tipped.

Closed, adamant shell –
you think of some girl, who has been waited for here;
who's come, at last, from church;

who is received in her cool,
coiffured whiteness. Like the shell,
underneath her that dark passage, and damp smell.

'The best place ...'

The best place to watch the rain
is from the window of an apartment building,
on the third floor,
looking across an empty sports field, at night.
Someone should have left those tall sodium lights on,
faintly lighting the rugby goals, in a real storm.
And there should be taller buildings about
with a few of their orange and yellow windows still burning,
balanced on blackness, in asymmetrical pattern.
By this light you'll see,
caught in a long drawn-out pleasure, the vast collapse
and sifting away of a whole mountain-stack
of new slippery straw –
the bleached silver, and frail pliant gold,
whirling off.
Or the rain is a headful of blond, loose hair
struck by wind,
flaring out, and drawn upon – as stirring as if
that's actually what you saw.
Growing heavier, the rain can seem not a rushing down at all,
in some lit places,
but a rapid oscillation, a flicker,
maintaining itself in mid-air.
The night as filled with rain as a plank with splinters.
Eventually, you turn inside, the long window left bared its full length,
and on a table is the typewriter, and the sawn block of white paper,
one sheet a curving grass-blade.
To the side in this room, in a smaller but similarly brazen window,
a tree-top is plastering,
thumping, and twisting itself about, like some enthusiastic postal
     clerk.
You sit down to the pleasure of writing when there is nothing that
     has to be written –
no article or review required; no editor
makes his pills ineffectual tonight
by chewing them with your name.
The desk lamp
curves its shadow across
all the shelved books, and they become
a crowd canopied in that vast South American football stadium,

whose voices now, in the midst of play,
you can no longer hear.
You're alone, the night before you.
The rain overwhelms itself outside. It is happiness.

Bondi

The waves are a shoal of white fins in the end of every downhill street,
and along the streets are stacked blunt-faced blocks of flats:
big, plastery, peeling buildings, in cream, with art deco curves and angles.
Behind this, for a thousand acres, the buckled suburbs of dark brick.
Curtains trail outwards on the heat, and a smell of gas leaks,
above singed grass in tiny yards, grey palings, chlorine-blue hydrangeas,
the gas pipes like creepers over walls.
There are garbage bins left lying about, empty milk bottles on marble steps,
always snail-dribble across the concrete, to the crushed snail shells.
The sun trundles around and around, amongst its flapping fire.
In the longest street, out toward the cave-in of the headland, is a children's park,
where, through empty swings, with their oversized hot chains, the surf swings.
Out here are callow home units of pale brick, fenestrated as the rock face
below the cliff's edge they're built upon.
Beyond a last railing, the sea flings out and spreads its crocheted cloth
across the rock table, and (something you can't watch for long, it is like madness)
draws it off, once again.
Around at the beach-front, rattling fun parlours, discos, and milk-bars, the sign-painting
lurid as tattoos, thickly over them.
Cars are tilted along all the gutters, strung together closely as caterpillars,
in the colours of children's sweets. The grit settles, coating
windscreens and duco; vinyl seats bake in the sun,

and that smell will sicken the overwrought children in the late
   afternoon, going home.
All day these headlands lie spread apart to the pleasurable,
   treacherous elements.
The place seems scoured by weather of every other ideal.
But then, a tall white yacht will appear in the ultramarine passage, an
   icon
of perfect adaptation, and the people along the sand,
as though in a grandstand, or those wading out
through the low waves towards it, seem all of them everywhere over
   this
like walking moths, that fan its easy passage with their wings.
It goes wandering on midway in the spectrum of blue before them,
   in the garment of serenity.
This is the only sort of vision we shall have, and it costs money,
and therefore Bondi is lying crammed together, obtuse, with barely
   a tree, behind us –
Every cent is firstly for the secure mechanisms of comfort.
It is not pleasure, to be exact, but its appropriation. And not
   mindlessness, but the mind.
For at the beach, so much that is nature can be seen to have been
   called
into the one procession of decay. Flesh become crude and brief
as figures shaped out of beach sand. So many of these people
look as though used like Bondi grit, with its scraps and butts and
   matchsticks.
Still, the young girls are loping on the sea-front, who secretly
amaze themselves with an easy skill they've found –
who can swing their breasts and all the shapes that are surging on
   their bodies
as if the drum majorettes for this parade.
At dusk, the parking spaces above the sea have emptied
and sand blows along the bitumen like smoke.
The garbage bins on posts are steep in their slipping litter.
And the gulls, that run and screech and scatter each other amongst
   it, never make
contented noises – are scrabbling constantly;
only sometimes one of them is carried off by the wind, down the
   bay, and it goes along
on its outriggers, smoothly; beautiful, particularly in the dusk,
when it flows away as smoothly, sideways, as the running shallows –
its whiteness, that is picked up by the whiteness of a wave's single
   wingbeat,
out there on the deep mauve water, creating a vast space.

Sketch of the Harbour

The long, wet trajectory of the ferry's railing
widely outswung
is safely caught in my hand.

And I watch a yacht that is coasting by,
at its bow the fumes
of a champagne bottle's lip.

All about on the harbour the yachts are slowly waltzing,
or in close-up
their ecstatic geometry.

Light fragments crackle above the suburbs and water,
whitely, as from a welder's torch,
on a soap-white day.

In the shadow of the ferry, the oily, dense water
is flexile, striated
as launching muscles.

But further out, there is only sunlight over a surface –
a constant flickering, like a lit-up
airport control.

And gulls, white as slung foam, glide alongside us here,
with the clear balloons of air
underneath their arms.

Emptying the Desk

Lastly, in the bottom drawer, a packet.
He breaks it open. And everything here feels the same as ever.
This had been the first time for him.
He recalls standing in that house, in mouldy darkness.
Rain collapsed outside
like a hurled net, the trees slashing and struggling underneath it.
His torch-beam, about the room,
was a trapped swallow.
He had hauled back the curtains, taking hold of their heavy moth fur.
No sign, that night, of the distant lit suburbs.
Dead flies along the window-sill, and hung inside an open jar.
And rain went on rushing smoothly into the earth
through one street light
the way the gleaming sides of an express train enter a tunnel.
He sees again the fence-eating grass,
and, like smoke drifting, a single car
that passed in the road.
There were some hobo's dirty blankets on a mattress, in one corner,
trodden against the wall;
a deal table, stained and burned; two overturned aluminium chairs;
newspaper everywhere. There was glass underfoot
from a broken-up, heavy sideboard.
He'd moved to the next room, stepping
along a slippery path. And in there, his torch-beam fell, almost at once,
on someone's eyes. It leapt, like a scorched finger.
He forced it back. His heart had stabbed downward through his
    bowels.
The torch-beam, he remembers, trembled
as if it were a water-light reflected indoors.
It was someone plainly dead.
And drying blood was everywhere, the way that vandals smear their
    shit about.
She wore some scrap of underwear,
and was like candle-wax; so delicate.
He has probably never, he realizes, for a whole day since then,
quite forgotten her.
Her feet were rolled open in a clown's walk,
her arms held downwards in the way
those young girls dance.
The blood, that made crazing all over her face,

was sticking underneath her head.
She'd seemed like porcelain – a shattered figurine, with an expression
horrified by what had happened to itself.
All this was a long time ago.
In some of these photographs white circles are drawn;
in others, the shape of her body has been traced on the dirty floor.
No more since then. He's often imagined
a room somewhere; 3 a.m.; rain dripping in the alley;
someone propped above her,
his brain haemorrhaging its pleasure. A need going on.
All these years, that her feet have only been running in a few scraps
    of heather;
and her mouth long since has been forced open
by the root of some decorous tree.
Outside, a summer afternoon.
The secretaries are coming back from lunch, along the drive,
or are sitting on the grass together.
In a corner, between two wings of the building,
there are a few nondescript small bushes, each of them only leaves,
and these are stirring slightly, on the end of the light.

Ten Poems

The curtains blowing
apart, a sock stretched open,
wide meadows.

Darkness, lake-hush;
a rowboat, allowed to drift, bumps
the starlight.

This moon, the last
tilted sauterne, in a glass
that's fire-lit.

A definition
of art deco: in black and cream
the butterfly.

Boiling water
poured from a saucepan
into a water-bottle's neck.
On the edge of your mind
the waves fall.

Wintry sunlight;
the dry, plastery legs of a woman
in tennis skirt.

A cathedral interior –
these long tapers of rain lighting
candles on the twilit river.

Wire coat-hangers,
misshapen, in a hotel wardrobe.
Steamy afternoon sun.

Cold swimming pool,
plastic blue. The bare tree's reflection,
its roots x-rayed.

Two magpies stepping
on the verandah. A ploughed hillside,
smoke, and cumulus.

A Day at Bellingen

I come rowing back on the mauve creek, and there's a daylight moon
among the shabby trees,
above the scratchy swamp oaks
and through the wrecked houses of the paperbarks;
a half moon
drifting up beside me like a jelly fish.
Now the reflected shapes are fading in the darkened rooms of the
    water.
And the water becomes, momentarily, white – magnesium burning.
My oars
have paused, held in their hailing
stance –
are melting;
and all the long water is a dove-grey rippled sand.
A dark bird hurries
low in a straight line silently overhead.
The navy-blue air, with faint underlighting,
has a gauze veil hung up within it, or a moist fresh smoke.
I land in the bottom of an empty paddock,
at a dark palisade
of saplings.
Among the ferns, dead leaves, fresh leaves, dry lightning-shaped
    twigs,
a cold breeze
comes up, rattling shreds all around.
A wind-blown star
is being drawn forth like a distant note.
The house I am the soul of lies,
hollow, on a ridge across the paddocks, although long occupied
    already
by the scouts of night.
I drag up the rowing boat, its rusty water slopping,
and start off, loosely in boots,
across the spongy, frog-bubbling undulations
of these coarse-bitten flats,
in a sharpened cow-dung smell.
After a day of sitting about,
spent reading and scribbling on margins
or bits of windy paper, and in remembrances,
the hours of which have passed

the way that water-drops fill at the downwards tip
of a twig,
I took the rowing boat out.
Rowed miles,
into the river, and downstream, over an ale-coloured brackishness –
through the societies of midges, in their visual uproar
(bronze-lit, like Caesar come to the Forum),
right out, equidistant from shore;
saw the birds swing on long trapezes across the green alcoves;
and followed all the notations of the tree-line
to those at dusk like flaking rust.
I came back with the slow-motion strides of a water spider over
    fluttered water.
As always, it has worked.
Now the mind is turned down, like a gas flame
in a dark kitchen,
where the wind and all the night sounds can again be heard.
It lies once more beneath the truth of the body.
All of my demanding
has become, crossing these paddocks, and watching the other stars
    appear,
as delicate as the first mould
on black bread, simply to take an axe and go on
up to the end of the cleared land, underneath the hooded eucalyptus
    forest,
to crack some firewood
from a weather-tightened grey log,
for a hot, deep bath, that I can draw out through the evening.

Landscape

    After the tide's long gear-shifting gesture,
    glimpsed among the bush,
    climbing down, toward ocean shallows'
    tilting opalescence.

    A washed sandbar, the yellow of a melon;
    rocks' wet terracotta;
    the viridescent cloud,
    sponge-pitted, that is crinkled weeds –

these are somewhere underneath the sluice
of cellophane-clear,
fast-drawn-off-the-roller, billowing
water, light-glistened.

Leaning above this, out of rock, angophoras –
a flesh-pink clamber
all over the dense ink blueness of the sky.
Trees like Schiele's posturing.

And two of them clash, their shadows clamped on
a single stone – leaping for the sun
with fingertips
that basketball players try to grow.

Bringing the Cattle

All afternoon I've lain about in this illuminated country, on one of the round hillsides, and have heard the squeak of cropped grass, and smelt the cow smell, like a warm convalescence, the cows close and oblivious, or with a sun-drugged interest.

 A hare stopped in the heat, and shivered, folding back its ears – the same way as the butterfly did its wings, on a plaited head of grass that hung above the ripe valley.

 But now the farmer, who all year wears shorts and rubber boots, and wades through the running shallows of paddock grass, who cracks his cattle with a stick across their bony out-crops, makes his voice float here.

 And the cows jolt down with everything swinging – the bellies, rounded as hammocks stretched full, and the four long teats, on udders that are grooved and furry like a peach.

 Their foreheads, between the big eyeballs' slow permanent surprise, make a wide, hollow-sounding target for the crowbar-wielding farmer when they've something broken or a germ.

 The hips, draped sharp Henry Moore shapes. And the splayed feet are placed with mincing care, as if they've high heels on.

Now a last cow is flouncing along the top of the slope, its spider-web fine thread of slobber blown out long in the final brightness of the sun.

The air is staining quickly with moisture, and the paddocks fill with vacancy.

These corridors lain across the beaten grass are alight and chill. The river, willow-shouldered, that was silk in the distance, now at twilight is all ice panels.

And the mist that will lie kerosene-blue and thick as smoke, through the night an incubus on creeks and dams, and that will drag among the raided, fluttering cornstalks, and stick the turned earth thickly, is already starting to seep from every dark socket of the ground.

So, following the cattle, and at their pace, I am also going down.

Karl Marx

Karl Marx was playing a parlour game
with his daughters. To their question
What is the quality one should most abhor?
he wrote: Servility.

This was found – a scrap of paper
amongst the family albums and letters;
it is the most essential of all
the Complete Works.

Watching by the Harbour

There is a late Sunday over the leaf-smoke suburbs.
The sidling of a candle snuffed
sets forth
above the burred metal plate of the bay.

And that smoke quickly becomes as frail and failing
in the strength of wintry light
as Oates
walking out alone into Antarctica.

Now the sky has paled like a butcher's clean shirt.
Far beneath it, a spread seagull
idly tries
its segments of a compass inscription.

Afternoon seems light that's escaping beneath a door.
In a cooling breeze the water shrivels
the same as flesh –
It happens mostly on the surface of the mind.

The plaster-thick paint of an end wall, in that hillside,
is gold-leafed, a moment, among
makeshift eucalypts.
Cattle-tracks of clear light trodden on the water.

At this reserve, the deep shadow of a ligamented fig,
a tilted lawn, the harbour set with sails
like restaurant tables.
Now early lights come out, smoky as lanterns.

'O time too swift, O swiftness never ceasing.' – This world,
it seems, is rattling in a gypsy's
hands, that part
and reveal how the things we love have gone.

The hills shall be valleys, and the valleys will be hills.
And someone who could drag open
a bow, in youth,
has fired away his life, lost with the arrow.

Fully dark; lit by distant hordes. And along the foreshores
you see now where there is nailed
a human warmth.
Our bivouac's encircled, in mountainous night.

Diptych

I

My mother told me how one night, as would often happen, she had
    stayed awake
in our wooden house, at the end of the dark
leaf-mulch of the drive,
waiting for my father, after the pubs had closed, knowing he would
    have to walk
miles, 'in his state',
if no one dropped him home,
since long before this he had driven his own car off a mountainside,
and becoming legend had rode
on the knocked-down banana palms
of a plantation, right to the foot, and someone's door,
the car reared high, and slipping fast,
on a vast
raft of mutilated, sap-oozing fibre,
from which he'd climbed down, unharmed, his most soberly polite,
and never driven again.
This other night, my mother was reluctant to go out, and leave us
    kids asleep,
and fell asleep herself, clothed, on the unopened bed,
but leapt upright, sometime later, with the foulest taste –
glimpsed at once
he was still not there – and rushed out, gagging,
to find that, asleep, she'd bitten off the tail
of a small lizard, dragged through her lips. That bitterness (I used to
    imagine),
running onto the verandah to spit,
and standing there, spat dry, seeing across the silent, frosty bush
the distant lights of town had died.

And yet my mother never ceased from what philosophers invoke,
    from 'extending care',
though she'd only ever read the *Women's Weekly*,
and although she could be 'damned impossible' through a few meal-
    times, of course.
This care for things, I see, was her one real companion in those
    years.
It was as though there were two of her,
a harassed person, and a calm, that saw what needed to be done, and
seemed to step through her, again.
Her care you could watch reappear like the edge of tidal water
in salt flats, about everything.
It was this made her drive out the neighbour's bull from our garden
    with a broom,
when she saw it trample her seedlings –
back, step by step, she forced it, through the broken fence,
it bellowing and hooking either side sharply at her all the way, and I
five years old on the back steps calling
'Let it have a few old bloody flowers, Mum.'
No. She locked the broom handle straight-armed across its nose
and was pushed right back herself, quickly, across the yard. She
ducked behind some tomato stakes,
and beat it with the handle, all over that deep hollowness of the
    muzzle,
poked with the millet at its eyes,
and had her way, drove it out bellowing; while I, in torment,
stood slapping into the steps, the rail, with an ironing cord,
or suddenly rushed down there, and was quelled, also,
repelled to the bottom step, barracking. And all,
I saw, for those little flimsy leaves
she fell to at once, small as mouse prints, amongst the chopped-up
    loam.

2
Whereas, my father only seemed to care that he would never appear
    a drunkard
while ever his shoes were clean.
A drunkard he would define as someone who had forgotten the
    mannerisms
of a gentleman. The gentleman, after all, is only known,
only exists, through manner. He himself had the most perfect
    manners,

of a kind. I can imagine no one
with a manner more easily, and coolly, precise. With him,
manner had subsumed all of feeling. To brush and dent the hat
which one would doff, or to look about, over each of us, and then
   unfold a napkin
to allow the meal, in that town where probably all of the men
sat to eat of a hot evening in a singlet,
was his passion. After all, he was a university man
(although ungraduated), something more rare then. My father, I see,
   was hopelessly melancholic –
the position of those wary
small eyes, and thin lips, on the long-boned face,
proclaimed the bitterness of every pleasure, except those of form.
He often drank alone
at the RSL club, and had been known to wear a carefully-considered
   tie
to get drunk in the sandhills, watching the sea.
When he was ill and was at home at night, I would look into his
   bedroom,
at one end of a gauzed verandah,
from around the door and a little behind him,
and see his frighteningly high-domed skull under the lamp-light, as
   he read
in a curdle of cigarette smoke.
Light shone through wire mesh onto the packed hydrangea-heads,
and on the great ragged mass of insects, like bees over a comb, that
   crawled tethered
and ignored right beside him. He seemed content, at these times,
as though he'd done all that he could to himself,
and had been forced, objectively, to give up.
He liked his bland ulcer-patient food
and the big heap of library books I had brought. (My instructions
   always were:
'Nothing whingeing. Nothing by New York Jews;
nothing by women, especially the French; nothing
translated from the Russian.')
And yet, the only time I actually heard him say that he'd enjoyed
   anything
was when he spoke of the bush, once. 'Up in those hills,'
he advised me, pointing around, 'when the sun is coming out of the
   sea, standing amongst
that high timber, you can feel at peace.'
I was impressed. He asked me, another time, that when he died

I should take his ashes somewhere, and not put him with the locals,
   in the cemetery.
I went up to one of the hills he had named
years earlier, at the time of day he had spoken of, when the half-
   risen sun
was as strongly-spiked as that one
on his Infantry badge,
and I scattered him there, utterly reduced at last, amongst the wet,
   breeze-woven grass.
For all his callousness to my mother, I had long accepted him.
After all, he'd given, or shown me, the best advice,
and had left me alone. And I'd come by then to think that all of us
   are pathetic.
Opening his plastic, brick-sized box, that morning,
my pocket-knife slid
sideways and pierced my hand – and so I dug with that one
into his ashes, which I found were like a mauvish-grey marble dust,
and felt that I needn't think of anything else to say.

Aubade

    The cold night that was clamped on the land
    falls loose, an unwound
    vise, and is lifted off.

    Light rises on the spider's web,
    the way that a needle-drawn thread
    is pulled through, to arm's length.

    The room is a bush clearing,
    a bale of light. A professional's grooming
    these curtains, as in their youth.

    And your long bright hair is like
    the first paint-loaded brush stroke
    that wanders before me over the white cloth.

Memories of the Coast

At times it could seem there was no life in the main street of a weekday,
and the road, going on, dipped beneath the sea.
A wind moved along the water there as though it were among grass tips,
beyond the tarred electricity wires, and the shoals and flat sheen of the bitumen.
We kids would come up from the beach onto four o'clock footpath heat –
hobbling barefoot and fast between awnings,
with our seawater towels, sand-chafing floppy shorts, zinc cream, spiked hair;
three or four of us, and dog – counting change,
once more, by the milkbar window's bleached posters and dead flies.
A brick side wall had a Bushell's sign as deeply blue as the sky.
On the way up, we came underneath a high paling fence, overhung with paspalum heads,
along a pathway of squeaking, flat-footed sand,
past some backyards – their woodpiles, cardboard boxes, lavatories, long weeds, wide underwear –
and off to the other side, a black railway goods yard;
coming out onto the shop fronts, that always looked half-witted, with their sun-in-the-eyes squint.
How poignant used to seem to me the beautiful, one-handed lady mannequin.
She was among bolts of cloth as big as papyrus rolls seemed on Sunday school cards.
We went reverently indoors, at Papandreou's –
to long floorboards, dusty air, the ice-cream scoops in a jar of milky water,
a dried shark's jaw,
flypaper so thickly used it was like a necklace of apple-pips,
chairs stacked on tables;
to a fifty year old bristled man who came chewing from out the back, the woman's side of it cut short,
for a threepenny-ha'penny sale.

At this time there were just a few fibro weekenders around, off
    among the sandhills' fluttered grass,
with watertanks on damp-rotted stands, flyscreens hung askew,
a rusty dog-chain stretched toward a puddle.
Behind those places, the slant, low trees seemed fused in a solid
    black clump,
coarse-leafed and sapless;
and when we came out from playing our games there, all through
    that sandy, speckled bush,
onto blue metal and dust at the level crossing,
we'd always see a few Aboriginals
going with a bottle to the sandhills, on flat pod feet.
Beyond the railway line, the one hotel's high verandah stood on
    insect legs, above the emollient of a pavement
that was constantly hosed, shifting dogs.
In the early fifties, most houses of town were sown loosely along
    the first few hillslopes
(before the mountains, that moved through every blue tone of iris
    petals,
back within the land's smoulder, that reversed sea-spray).
The dusty streets had mainly weatherboard places
on low posts; no pavement or kerb, but each bungalow with its
    concrete front path,
and silvered steep roofing iron,
and 'chook' run and rhubarb in the backyard.
At St John's, there'd often be a heifer browsing, biblically,
just outdoors from the baptismal font;
and inside, someone had told me once, there was a fisherman laid
    out, all his flesh
green-bearded with dangling prawns.
Most of the houses then looked over the shops, and the ply-mill
    smoke, over the muscle-building
bend of the Coast railway line,
over the tiles of the school; the listless rugby goalposts, near grassy
    sandhills,
the afternoon drizzle on the ziggurats
of peeled eucalyptus poles,
the Melanesian-looking spindly construction of the long jetty with
    its crane,
the gull-molested fishing boats,
the timber boat, being slowly trodden down, before disappearing,
and the estuary, that often held an ochre sandbank
of perfect river-pebble shape –

looked out across the ocean, that was momentarily changing, and
   too huge to really look at, stretching the mind apart.
All of that is gone now, of course, under concrete flats and shops,
   car-parks, and a highway;
even the sea has been largely blocked out –
we shall sleep no more.
And I am like a salmon, that can't forget the place where it was born
and only wants to return there. Nowhere
is like that any longer.

What I most often remember now, of all that time,
is just one afternoon. I had come home early from school, on my
   own, and my mother called me
to get the washing in.
Clouds were coming up like the Zulu tribes.
And it seemed such a big deal, to be helping your mother in this
   way, when she was excited –
she was flying along the clothes-line, plucking leaf and flower.
There was the train's whistle
from the shunting yard. I carried everything –
it was bundled into a sheet, and slung across my shoulder. The first
   raindrops,
blown, I told myself were spears
all around me, as I was jerked about, and bounced, running up the
   backyard. Some big splattered wounds,
but I made it
onto the back porch. Getting dark in there, behind the trellis,
where leaves were scraping. And she spoilt it all,
by throwing inside a floorcloth, and a ragged bathmat, and running
   out into battle again
for the peg box – which I'd have done. She came back soaked,
   soaked all over,
in a suddenly steaming rain. No one could have survived it –
I dropped that game, not to think of such a thing.

For Harriet

A pewter-coloured,
atomized steam

is left in the early, sunlit
bathroom,

and there the child has made
a cameo

of privacy. I pass
that smoke-breathing

doorway, and see how she has stepped
down

into the fields of women;
stooped

with hair-brush
to the first harvest

of her
uncertain pleasures.

At the Inlet

In the dawn an eagle leaves the forest; now the flat sea is lichened with the sun. The fish will be sparks of darkness, pouring through the water. And those thick-fingered long wings cup and undulate, loose and watery on the air.

Thus nature maintains itself without my concurrence; before it all my subjectivity has no standing and is dissolved. In taking it to myself, I find an incomparable satisfaction.

While the surrealists, who sought the Marvellous, that is hidden somewhere within us, have produced only the grotesque. How detestable, their facile sacrifice of the beauty which things have –

The dust on a sunlit window-pane; the life of the pores, of the hairs along the shin; the globed moisture on the upper lip; and the nipple, made of little packed, flattened globes, like a boysenberry, unripe pink. Inevitable that I should think of D., 'the bird of loudest lay' ...

I've opened the petals on the bud in her flesh. Branches ache around the powdered moon; contralto stars. She arches on her back; her face is soaring; her breasts seem wind-compacted. The lights of a town across the bay, like the broken streamers of our departure. And the salty snail-glitter of stars down the glass.

Is this world of ours being scattered, the flying rubble from burst Paradise? So my mother taught, but I can only believe it when overlong in the cities, amongst other men.

Nature, in Chinese thought, is the creator of itself. It is not necessarily benign or hostile to man, who is just a part, and must find his place within its being. The name of that teaching is sanity.

A ladle has been hung by the open kitchen window. Forest, ocean, sky.

With the natural object, an artist has all he needs to express himself. This dictum of Pound's was foreseen by Aristotle: Nothing in the mind that isn't first in the senses. Therefore, it can be said that a life's fulfilment is in the contemplation of matter.

The true nature of the world is not different to the things we see. 'You should not cling to an essence that is separate from the outside of things. When someone sees mountains and rivers, he sees the Buddha-nature: when he sees the Buddha-nature, it is the cheeks of a donkey or the mouth of a horse.'

An early morning sea with a row of streetlights burning, a bare railway platform, and a few late stars. All that has beauty in human experience only exists in this way because of death. And the nothingness of death is not so vast or terrible; it is more like something intimate. It's of my size, exactly.

Since the ego of an individual can be shown to be an illusion (which we experience as estrangement and lifelessness), any philosophy that finds an ego in the universe – God, or some abiding Absolute – reinforcing, and arising out of, such illusion, must itself be equally false.

The fibrous grasses that grow sparsely across the sandhills flicker. If grass were measured on a scale beside water, this would be a trickle from rusty pipes. And the broken palings of the back fence are plaited with old bloodied strands of wire. The fence sags full of sand, and yet is eloquent as a mainsail, in its curving before the sea.

Mr Nelson

Their house was old grey weatherboards, on a small town back-street
of shale and potholes and white dust;
the porch in lattice
from which some last off-white paint was almost gone.
It was down a slope,
with high posts in the back, blue hydrangeas
along the front, and it had two concrete steps, and a steep, gravel-
   rashed iron roof.
The picket fence was unpainted, also,
tall paspalum
growing amongst it, where the scythe or push-mower couldn't reach.
I used carefully to pull a long, pale strand
of that round grass
from deep in its coarse outer sheaths, not breaking it, but getting a
   very long
curved frond, and would lightly
touch my mother's arm

with the asymmetrical head, while she was talking over the fence
    there,
so we could go on.

Almost all of the houses on that sunlight-dragged, smoke-idling
    street
were alike, except those with louvres
above their verandah sides, or a faded canvas blind.
A few newer places, in fibro,
had flat roofs, and were painted
with army surplus undercoat, pink or aquamarine.
Where some young people lived
there'd be an old car in the front yard, its parts seemingly always
    spread on the grass,
and a wireless playing loudly from indoors.
The songs I'd hear,
my forehead leaned against the fence, while flattening an ants' nest
    with my shoe,
or trying to heap it up again,
were things like 'Ghost Riders in the Sky', and 'The Streets of
    Laredo',
and 'Half As Much':
If you lo-ved me halfasmuch as I love you,
You wouldn't st-ay a-way halfasmuch as you do,
sung by a whiny female voice.

Along the top of the low, cleared hills, behind those deep backyards,
there was some remaining bush, and this
used to seem so dreary,
like the old cooking-splatters and fly-specklings of a kitchen wall.

Mrs Nelson would come out
to talk with my mother over the fence;
small and dried up,
with a voice like little bundles of twigs snapping and giving.
She was nervous-eyed as a hen,
and had a very hollow throat, inside its slack strings.
Her teenage daughter had been killed by a car
when riding a bike,
and so my mother always used to speak of Mrs Nelson as 'that poor
    thing'.

Standing at their front gate, making the latch click open and shut,
    gently,
careful not to be told, in mid-conversation, to get away,
or to have my hand slapped,
I could look down into their door and through the house, out to the
    bright-lit,
bleached backyard, with its long sapling clothes-line poles
that held up tea-towels, sheets, and bloomers.
And I'd sometimes see Mr Nelson's shape,
his prolapsed stomach, in the blue singlet he always wore,
crossing their kitchen, at the end of the hall. Barefoot on the lino,
    he carried
a teapot and newspaper,
or half a loaf of bread on its board, or a tin of jam
with open, serrated top. Sometimes he'd come out
and offer me a Ginger Nut biscuit, if he saw me looking through
    the gate-slats,
and then he'd say, just a bit more loudly,
'Your copper's boiling.'
He seemed a peculiar man,
diffident even with a child, and so polite and embarrassed with my
    mother.
He had a broad, cracked face, with what I see now
as a glaze of grief over it,
that had seemed then like a feeling of sickness, in the light,
and so I suppose I'm remembering him from shortly after his
    daughter's 'accident'.

One time my mother told me, after we'd left their gate and were
    hurrying on,
going to visit my grandparents around the corner, something else
about the Nelsons.
– I don't know what Mr Nelson's job was, although I remember
he once wore black sump-oil boots,
but he evidently could walk home through the cemetery,
at the end of their street, where the daughter was buried,
and he must have got off early, as Council workers do, because this
    happened
in hot afternoon sun.
(I've seen the cemetery there at such a time:
glary marble along the hill, amongst orange clay and grey, poor
    grass,
underneath a sudden cliff-face of dark bush,

with cicadas shrilling
in the heat, so loud they made your head feel
it was being spun rapidly within.)
Among those dusty, bleached-out plastic flowers, and the jars of
 black water,
Mr Nelson had come on a large brown snake, the venomous type,
curled in the sun, on a grave-top.
He'd looked for something to kill it with, creeping off,
and had only been able to grab a bit of rusty iron fence
from a sunken grave, that he could work loose, that had
lumps of concrete sticking to it,
and he struck with this –
but the metal was awkwardly bent, he was hitting onto
the hill below, and the snake
had sensed him, so that even though he swung several times, it got
 away,
into a hole down the side of someone's grave.
The trouble was, he'd been seen
from a distance, seemingly smashing about,
by a person who had gone and told the minister, who'd
inspected, and told the police, and so on. That bit of rail
was decorated and barbed, and had scratched the headstone's face
as he tried to bash close beside it. Mrs Nelson said to Mum
that for the damage he'd caused
they were being sued by someone or other, a big noise in town,
and they had no money,
with the funeral expenses, recently. My mother was 'very sad', and
 annoyed,
over this happening at such a time 'to that poor woman'.

When I was about fifteen, with a taste for Romantic poetry,
I used to wander around in the graveyard sometimes – my
 grandparents were there by then –
where I once found
a heavily scratched and chipped headstone. (Perhaps the case
 against Mr Nelson had been lost,
or the money was used for something else.) And I could work out,
mainly with my fingertips,
that there'd been a particularly unctuous verse, something about
God wanting the best early, for Himself,
once carved upon it.

Curriculum Vitae

1
Once, playing cricket, beneath a toast-dry hill,
I heard the bat crack, but watched a moment longer
a swallow, racing lightly, just above the ground. I was impressed by
   the way
the bird skimmed, fast as a cricket ball.
It was decided for me, within that instant,
where my interests lay.

And the trajectories at dusk of random moths and lone decisive
   swallow
will often still preoccupy me, until dew occludes the air.

2
I can remember there were swallows that used to sew together
the bars of a cattle yard.
I would be sitting in morning sunlight
on the top rail, to feel its polished surface
beneath my hands.
A silvery, weathered log that had the sheen of thistle's flax.

3
A cow was in the stocks with the calm expression of a Quaker;
and my father stretched his fingers,
a pianist seated on a chopping block. He bent his forehead to an
   instrument
out of Heath Robinson –
a dangling bagpipes, big as a piano,
that was played by tugging on organ stops.
The cow began to loosen its milk: its teats were disgorged,
the size and colour of small carrots;
and milk was flourished in the bucket, two skewer-thin daggers
sharpened on each other underhand.
Then, as the bucket filled, there would be the sound of a tap running
into deep suds at the end of a bath.
Finally, the calf was let in,
and this sounded like a workman building-up a big lather between
   his hands.

The concrete in those bails was shattered, but lay together
as though a platform of river stones; and water ran there constantly
from a hose, breaking up and bearing off
the hot lava of any cow-pats. That water was delicate and closely-
    branched –
a long weed fluttering, on such a breezy morning.

4
There were great dents of cloud-shadow on the blue-forested
    mountain;
and far off, over
the paddocks, through midday heat, the fluttering silk scarf
of a light purple range.
Our mountain was the kite, and those in the distance, its tail,
through all the heat-wavering days.
And many broken, dead trees had been left standing about,
like stone ruins: pillars that held out the remnants
of cloisters and fine stonework,
with rubble beneath them. But the air was so clear; so uncrowded
with any past –
arbitrary corridors, unpeopled, through the air.
Room for the mind to travel on and on.
I used to have to stop, often, to stand there, in that immense
    amphitheatre
of silence and light.

5
I remember watching our three or four geese let loose and rushing,
with their heads beating sideways like metronomes,
towards a dam where the mountain-top hung;
and when they entered the water, the mountain's image came apart
suddenly, the way a cabbage falls into coleslaw.
Everything was changed, as easily as that.

6
Since then, I have been, for instance, in Petticoat Lane – pushing by
through narrow, stacked alleys,
among the tons of rotting garbage for sale,
and have seen the really poor.
Those people seemed just dangling paper dolls, threaded onto
a genetic string –

the characters of poverty, starch, lack of sun,
and stunted, hopeless spirit everywhere. Their crossed eyes,
twisted faces, snaggle teeth,
drunkenness were Dickens still, in '70 something,
again in '82. – People in greasy rags, on crutches, weeding wet butts
from the gutters;
spiky-haired, furtive, foul-muttering.
The women were shaped like slapped-together piles of clay. They scrabbled
amongst junk, viciously,
yelling to each other, and oblivious....

What is such an evil, but the continuing effect
of capital's Stalinism?
Enclosure, as John Clare has said, lets not a thing remain.

And then, an hour later, in the West End I found
how much worse I thought an askance,
meringue-coloured, prissy-lipped upperclass face – so sleek
in its obliviousness.
People go rotten with culture, also.

7
Another time, in Washington, when my girlfriend had gone
to see someone,
and while I was sitting at an upstairs window, I watched the bald man
who lived next door, after he'd argued once more
with his wife, come out to stand alone
in their backyard – round as a pebble, in his singlet,
but nowhere near so hard.
He was standing with chin sunk,
holding the garden hose – a narrowed stream
he felt around with
closely, like a blind man's cane.
It disturbed me to see him like that – and then, as I started to consider myself,
I saw that I was walking
in those silver paddocks, again,
which as a kid I'd known.

8
Or travelling alone in Europe once, and staying in a provincial city,
indolent and homesick of an afternoon,
I turned, as ever, to the museum.
In such a mood, however, the masterpiece will often no longer serve:
it seems too strenuous and too elevated;
it belongs in a world too far beyond one's own.
From experience, one has learned at these times to follow that
    arrow, *École française*
XIXe siècle. There, on an attic floor,
unnoticed by the attendant, a newspaper crumpled
over his boots, or along the deserted outer corridors,
beneath tall windows, in the light from which
many of them are cancelled,
hang one's faithful mediocrities – in sympathy with whom
one had thought to be borne through until dinnertime.
Armand Guillaumin, Léon Cogniet, Jules Dupré, Félix Ziem:
no artistic claims can be made for these. Their sluggish or
    bituminous pigment,
greasy sheen, and craquelure,
their failures, so complex and sad, have earned them
'an undisturbed repose'.
And yet, even these harmless,
unassuming, and forgotten, as I glanced among them, on this
    occasion,
were forgotten
by their one idle, arbitrary re-creator,
and the landscapes that came far more vividly before my eyes
were all memories.

9
Into my mind there has always come, when travelling,
images of the twisted Hawkesbury bush
crackling in the heat, and scattering its bark and twigs about,
white sunlight flicked
thickly on the frothy surges
and troughs of its greenery; and within those forests,
great pools of deep fern, afloat
beneath a sandstone rock-lip; and of the Platonic blueness
of the sky; and recollections of Coledale and Thirroul
on their clifftops, where sea-spray
blows among the pines and eucalypts; and, most of all, of those
    forests,

cool, light-flouncing, with white female limbs,
and of the yeasted green pastures,
where my mind first opened, like a bubble from a glass-blower's tube,
and shone, reflecting
things as they are –
there, where I have felt, anxiously, I would find them
a while longer,
after passing Kempsey, once more, on the mail train of an early morning.

Piano (1988)

Black Landscape

All of the high country, that year, had been burned out
with the headline blackness of war.
Soon afterwards we came travelling through the place,
along a ridge's blade-edge, by car.

The tree-forms then were the crudest of hieroglyphs –
a crushed charcoal scrawl;
petrified in their extreme gesturing, about those hills
steep as a landslide sprawl.

Rain-storms had just been there; in overcast light
boulders exuded shine.
And the clinkered valleys were backed with high, wet cliffs.
An immense open-cut coal mine.

We were creeping through winds that pounded on the car;
twanged it; made it a cripple;
that seemed to compress its shape. But stopped to photograph;
the car was braced like a mule.

Climbed down, into stillness and deadness. The clay slopes'
squirming runnels, closely traced,
left earth hung between horizontal strata – a Hindu façade,
now almost effaced.

A crow was blown away, with a shout; I thought of having to eat
such dry fibre. Keats didn't know
all about those syllables, 'forlorn', who'd never heard
a sound like the bushfire's crow.

Everywhere, great ruptured webs, the shining charcoal bushes.
Twigs traced and smudged us black.
I saw ahead, in profile, how a cliff-face was built of shale:
the silverfishes' newspaper stack.

Smell of wet ashes, and trickling of water. We found
headless trees breaking there
into fine leaves, again: the boles were stockinged with them
as with flame. A tremulous mohair.

In red and green of an apple. So: fire, air, water, earth;
each contending with another;
shifting of energies, as animals shove in their sleep. And life,
too, where things are sore.

I took from beneath a stone the cicada: six-legged tottering;
three clear jewels on its brow;
a samurai's orange mask. Those beautiful gauze wings
segmented with a gum tree bough.

Between such branches, if you tilt your hand, you can make
a light, pale blue and frail
as after sunset. I told a girl once, in Ireland, of cicadas;
she said, 'We only ever had a snail.'

A Port of Europe

Like a bandage in a gorse bush, water gleams
on the dark-clouded moor,
and far off, in the other direction, along the top of the world,
lies a slat of metal ocean, under
brittle moonlight.
The moon is resonant on the sea, as though a gong-face were flicked
with a fingernail;
and one dark, cowled farmhouse, with chalky jowls, drowses
stiffly here, in a hallway for the winds –
it is the nun who keeps a door.
Westward from Flensburg, on these low marshlands
of saturated green,

air capers wildly
as children of the poltergeist,
vaulting far over the metronome monotony of windmills, and the
   few small startled horses
with wind-hacked manes.
The shoreline and fields are mere sediment of the coagulating sky.
The ocean shifts as though weight-lifted oil,
and under old jetties undulates
lubriciously as crazed inmates on the poles.
Black outer waters of ocean jostle
and bound, a herd of migrant tusks, that mills and advances again,
and fills one with dread, imagining
the blankly inhuman nature
of a primal force.
A small town flies the moon with its flags,
among casques of verdigris. The landscape stares in, down the
   streets,
and carries within its cloak
the cock of mockery.
Spires and clock-chimes, and beneath them a few sails
cupped and pulsing softly, like pale jelly-fish;
and long water-logged barges
that burrow in the deep grey or moss-black estuarine waters.
Over the acres of sea-front, dieseline
and urinous salt. Here, the parlours of casseroles and geraniums,
of alcohol, onion-rings, pipe smoke,
and old fish-nets dried as roots. A patina of human grease
is on every stone and sill. And these scratched, pewter-coloured
   faces –
are these the heads of tragic clowns,
or snouts, in trampled water?
The clouds at sunset were vast, lurid fungi:
damp purples, yellows, and vermilion. One sail
like a drifting spore –
the long-tailed seed of a pine cone, that had burst in a distant fire –
was wavering there,
towards what seemed the mountainous country of the sky;
but it will have fallen again
upon this shore.

Very Early

Birds are drifting, bubbles on the eyesight, in a frangipani sunrise.
Waves nod as a rocking horse would,
if it were one that left standing before long windows could
stir with the air. Now on the bay lies
the diamond flotilla. And right the length of the harbour
a light stretches, that's one duellist, and the other.

Or the weavings of an immediate Penelope. And now, a vast trunk
 of light,
speckled about with a leaf-shimmer
of light-points. On many a verandah
you see where the summer mist of the mosquito net
is still abroad. The hypotenuse at ease.
Curlicues on a dog's back are being planed by a breeze.

The dog, tongue loose as a pocket hanging out,
is leaving the reserve (these roman candles of green,
the lawns pebbly with dew, and moored yachts with their bathroom
 sheen);
it blows away into the open barn door of a street –
dimly and complacent, follows a hunch.
A small, dark bird in there shifts like a sparkle on a branch.

Here at the park, a turbaned snail, the potentate of the dew,
majestically moves. Gum leaves are eyebrows being drawn
on light. A spider hangs in the midst of dawn.
The pine trees, at a distance, seem water-stains down a plastery blue.
If no one saw all this, its existence would go on just as well.
And what is really here no words can tell.

Rainy Windows

Wildly flourished, little pods of water;
and these long runnels, drawn among them, for the stalks –
it is a frieze of shivery grass.

A puffed diffidence, of floaty, pattered weeds.
Or a carbonated glass, in which the apothegmatic bubbles
are pressured down.

Through gauzy water, gate-posts,
tiles, chimneys, black tentacles, and the sudden leaf-twitches
of birds leaping, without birds.

The pavement twitches. Out there,
the land of 'the Anthropophagi, and (of those) whose heads do grow
beneath their shoulders'.

Across my room, a window's lizard skin,
silverish-grey. Then, going over, the world is in all the jumbled
colours, and fogginess, of a wok.

One keeps returning: to what's also the smudge
on chilled white grapes. Within it, the light of a chardonnay.
Approached, a fluttery veil – frail

and dotty. A Zelda Fitzgerald, though one
calmer now. This tender collector of sodden lengths of string.
Along the road, soda fuzziness

as lights appear in late afternoon.
It has all become a watercolourist's first essay, washed off
beneath the tap. A miscegenated grey.

In such weather, only largeness matters,
bases endure. The watcher's allowed an intimation of release
in the detachment of this flickery change.

I always find with such weather an utter
accord. As when, grown still, one lies sidelong to consider
the perspiring face of one's love.

Byron Bay: Winter

Barely contained by the eyesight,
the beach makes one great arc –
blue ranges overlap behind it;
each of them a tide-mark.

About me, swamp-oaks' foliage
streams, hatching by Cézanne.
Off in the heath, a guard's carriage
follows the vats of a train.

A creek spoils the hem of the sea;
spread on the beach in flutes
it has the redness of black tea,
from the swamp's sodden roots.

Behind, cloudy afternoon swells,
the colour of claret stain.
The sunlit town is strewn like shells.
Its lighthouse, a tiny pawn.

I'm walking on the beach alone;
the sea's grey feathers flurry,
showing emerald. Sandpipers blown
seem mice, in their scurry.

And the sun on my shoulders brings,
because it's perfect warmth,
the feeling that I wear great wings
while stepping along the earth.

A Garden Shed

From ten to thirteen I was often sent
for a month or even more at a time
to my grandmother's in a distant town
after grandfather died – it was thought
I should go, though she hardly spoke.

I read by the stove; she would pause
in sewing, sometimes, and you'd see
she was out billowing about, or
crouching beside doors along the night,
pushing at some. I kept a watch;

but after school I used to wander
in the scrub behind that big-verandahed,
shabby, dislocated bungalow, beyond
her call and the other straggling houses
at the town's edge; and I saw how

once in the country the train began
wildly careering, with its horn
braying out, again and again.
When I arrived first, rain appeared:
long slashes on a carriage window

that broke up those trajectories,
so the heavy glass it seemed was chipped
at, but slowly – too slowly for escape.
I remember the clattering of a tocsin,
the railway crossing that we burst

right through – a clown and hoop;
and I was driven on, landed, lips stretched,
on my feet. It must have been
the ache at her house was the boredom,
since it was never really so good

being at home. But the mountains between,
above small-town, dairy farm smoke,
were a kingfisher blue, and their glint,
coming from night, was sad like a sail
that passes by. Strange you don't complain

at that age. I'd the inarticulate
endurance children have, or some have.
Grandma died of her strokes, completely mad.
I only liked there when allowed the key
to grandfather's shed. 'Just so's to look.'

At the end of a long, overgrown yard,
past lumber on trestles, the chicken run
of oil-black earth and wire netting,
the tatty eucalypts with their clothes line,
all in a high stockade of palings,

I let myself in. There, I'd rediscover
each chisel, peculiar saws, the claw
and ballpein hammers, his screwdrivers,
brace-and-bits, punches, spanners, and
a regal, African paint brush array,

stood on shakily-done shadowboards –
things spiky, knobbed, sharp or frayed
like those raced among, beyond the fence,
out on the heath. I'd handle these,
but it would have been sacrilege for me

to think them useable. (It was there
I was betrayed, my family would say.)
All of that was carefully hung,
sharp and oiled, in the gloom again,
with glints – strange, like creatures in

(were it possible) a deep-sea aquarium.
And I found beneath the workbench
sawdust still adrift in a spider's web.
There was an old sofa, brown, bleached
as though a rose petal in a book;

and stacks of bevelled, collected timber
slung overhead – how curious those
differing lengths: each had a meaning,
I felt, like poetry-shapes to be read
some day in our maroon leather Milton.

Grimy light in there made it look
always a rainy afternoon. In the quiet
I could hear the neighbour's hens creak
just outside, or the washing flap,
or a car somewhere, changing gear.

And I've always wanted to live again
at the level where one lived when
looking at, or listening to, those things:
in the immense presence of a wordless
questioning. I seemed to be lying alone

out on a hillslope, until I could hear
coming through things cast-up about there
a far roaring, of their endless sea.
In the secret noise of such turmoil
and spray, I was somehow looking back –

or being looked through, about to be lost –
to my grandfather and I, who were only
bubbles of a moment, amid this whirling
away. I first recognized the frankness
of nature's appropriations there:

that it's all effectiveness, inter-response;
all mutuality and possibilities;
just things happening among themselves.
Things creating each other. And we
are only the expressions of circumstance,

of its tensions. Nothing belongs to any
separate thing. It was there I began
to understand: the less we think we are
the more we bear; and someone who sees
he is nothing, lightly will bear it all.

Harbour Dusk

She and I came wandering there through an empty park,
and we laid our hands on a stone parapet's
fading life. Before us, across the oily, aubergine dark
of the harbour, we could make out yachts –

beneath an overcast sky, that was mauve underlit,
against a far shore of dark, crumbling bush.
Part of the city, to our left, was fruit shop bright.
After the summer day, a huge, moist hush.

The yachts were far across their empty fields of water.
One, at times, was gently rested like a quill.
They seemed to whisper, slipping amongst each other,
always hovering, as though resolve were ill.

Away off, through the strung Bridge, a sky of mulberry
and orange chiffon. Mauve-grey, each cloven sail –
like nursing sisters in a deep corridor, some melancholy;
or nuns, going to an evening confessional.

Eight Poems after Kusadao

two
things

that have
no

memories

fresh

fallen
snow

a

leaping

squirrel

—

at
dawn

three or
four

often

to say
they're

wronged

—

cutting
at

the
cabbage

heart

and
a rooster

calls
far

off

in
huge

desolation

—

my
wife

two
nights

gone
for

two
nights

the
galaxy

—

a
plum

bloom
trodden

down
shows

us
this

earth

—

late
night

apples
lamp-

lit
stall

and
Orion

in glory

—

zazen
in

temple
cold

so
harsh

my
eyes

trickle
hopeless

longing

—

autumn

I
hear

cicadas
grow

fainter

with
no

resistance

Nakamura Kusadao, haiku poet, 1901–1984.
Translated with Professor Shigeo Kitagawa, Tokyo, 1985.

Plurality

To Philip Hammial, the traveller from an antique land

Our flat was in a building which backed onto the golf course,
and it shone with the bay. In this street,
hosannas of Mediterranean palms, and Moreton Bay fig trees
pressing large fingers to the light.
There we lived, day after day.

A concrete esplanade, planted with old metal lamp-posts,
shaped the waterfront. The bay's wobble
when the tide was running in
was like the filled reboundings of a spirit level.
Or the water grey and heavy as a punt.

This also had its beauty. If a tug or trawler came
from under leaves, on such a day,
the bow-wave was luminously white. And gangly yachts,
subtly restless, as though they were a schoolgirls' assembly,
waited – their gowns, umbrellas rolled tight.

Out in the harbour, along the moored steamers' high black sides,
drifting up and down, dropping like shuttles
down a spindle, levered up again – for their tensile
wide-orbiting dance – were gulls.
The dreaming efficiency of machine parts, in the distance.

From our windows late, with lights out, the water shimmering
as if leaves on a tree,
the way it was lifted in the moonlight. And further on, toward
the moon, the harbour so gauze-like it could be
a desert – untrodden, silvery-dewed.

This was, for me, the tranquil early eighties; I was not yet forty.
I've mostly lived near the sea;
part of my boyhood was remote, in the face of empty water.
I think at the end we live a similar way.
In those days, it was on a headland, yellow and dusty.

The tall sea could seem, at once, a wall and its isolate
forbidden garden. (O fertile, impossible sea.)
The earth there, with a scumbling of tight grass, was in the summer
zwieback. A few weatherboard houses, dry
as folds of a lizard's throat, before the jangled light.

Washing waved to nothing. Our side wall transformed
in late afternoon, like a filled sponge. For play, as a kid,
I'd a myriad small antheaps – their energy of boiling saucepans.
The clouds often like a motorcycle skid.
Beyond the stale mustard-colour of land, a ship went traipsing.

Quartz gravel, dandelions, rusty tin, the blown
dirt road, slant telephone poles, a reservoir....
Then, below our flat, someone swaying on a moisturized golf-
    course
beside the bay, posed like a figurine for us to admire.
I don't forget the real nature of the ocean.

If you live with that, and little else, it will come to seem a dream
that is fed with dreams. It deals, then keeps on and on
to regain. It's both good and evil
and will not resolve itself where you draw a line.
Long fumbling to describe it, I heard of the sky burial.

In Tibet, when someone ordinary dies, because the earth is sacred,
and there's such scarcity of wood,
they're laid on a large rock outside town, where an undertaker,
with two knives, goes to work – the body is dissected;
the skin flayed, all joints severed.

Male relatives watch from a short distance those gesturing tools
of a little squatting monkey, whom no one
but outcasts will speak to, whom no doctor will treat,
his white robes growing silently spoiled. He has slit the body open
and piles the organs like jewels.

Briskly scores and dices flesh; takes a small sledge-hammer
to the bones, pounding each one;
he makes of the whole body, within three-quarters of an hour,
a neat wet pile. No pictures of this can be taken.
Into bones and flesh stirs some barley-meal.

Finally stands back, and holding wide his hands, stiff as prods,
those two weird flowers, he sings,
ululates, to the eroded escarpments around, the one extraordinary
word, of Tibetan knife-carved lettering, that brings
thumping about him an avalanche of big, loose clods –

The vultures amble over each other's backs, and slap
monstrous gloves. Saved for the leader of the flock,
now thrown him, the liver. Trampling of waves. And these great
   wings
glisten and stream. In minutes, not a sliver on the rock.
Their flight: graceful and horrible. It cancels out.

There is nowhere valuation. Everything, equally, is desire to live.
It is a oneness, always plural.
Yet, if someone crosses the stale ditch about themselves,
or the yachts on blueness incarnate a breeze, or a face is beautiful,
how this ocean's endless hunger can seem worthwhile.

Walking Around at Night

The rising moon appears,
softly focused as a movie queen,
in a close frame
through the kitchen fly-screen.

I stroll outside, and down the path,
leaving a radio;
the moon is buxom
above the smokily-draped willow.

It's soon the old fumy paraffin lamp
of a moon, that I prefer.
The hammer blows of barking,
a car clearing its chest, somewhere,

the slam of a tinny garage door
on concrete, and the voices
going inside, that could be either quarrelsome
or boisterous.

A torn white paper edging
of water in the gutter.
The poplars and bushes, that wait for me to pass,
are dressed in *purdah*.

This dim-lit town backs
into black gullies, from the milkbar freeway;
a few novas burn
in the shapeless dusty galaxy.

The white-painted boards of some houses
wear a net veil
of leaf-shadows. These lawns, side-lit,
are wheatgrass: succulent, shapely, and frail.

The parking lot is bare tonight
within a cold, immense
chain-wire, on which I lean. The shadows of some pebbles
loom like a chess defence.

This way, just out of town, is a tall hill-shape –
a dark, perfect dune –
unravelling irregularly as coarse cloth
its outline, under the moon.

Across the paddocks, backyards –
above the fences, lounge room lights burn;
in the frosty night, thick like thistle fur,
a few porch lights are on.

I keep walking, and see that a cow and the moon
are each a term
in some kind of sequence. I shoo
a cow up, for a place to lie that's warm,

under a lichen-smoke and bird's egg sky.
Adrift on the frothy night.
It gets chill. Going on, toward a razor-strop highway –
that sound, those streaks of light.

They are suddenly lifted away at the curve
and gone – each a stroke;
and there's an occasional heavy flat backward
stropping, that is a truck.

Waiting to cross (a short-cut back), I stand off
in the weeds. At every car,
these are strung with glutinous, distended drops.
The moon's blue as an old scar.

Prunus Nigra

The plum tree with popcorn blossom
is pink upon the frost,
or it's embossed on the dusty blueness
of the lower sky, toward dusk.

A magpie, ragged witch-doctor,
long-jumps to the clothes-line pole;
behind it, the plum tree bursts
like a wave at sunset.

How terrible it would be
if this plum bloomed near the palings
and one saw it with the memories
of some other life.

Fire Sermon

Now the lissome bay is silvered slightly, in its supine lightness;
a stocking-textured water
takes the morning's cerise.

But soon, between headlands, the gradation of blue, mirrored,
that has closed almost
seamlessly, like stone.

And yachts have come out to climb along the sea's face, slow
and wavering – the way
that cabbagemoths walk.

These foreshores are deeply tented with pines and eucalyptus
and tea-trees, leaning
on the engorged light.

It's here the cicadas' sizzling, strapped toffee strings of sound,
filmy and flashing, fuse
into sheets, all around.

And here those rhythmical light-points shoal the water thickly
as the shift to shovelled
gravel in cicadas' song.

Simmered eucalyptus oil's vaporously uncoiled, accompanying
angophoras, dancing
Indras of rosy stone.

Dilated summer: it seems you see into the Flame, as light-cells
teem, cicadas thrum – to
its naked, sensuous events.

On the far shore, a few houses are hung, white muslin among
bush humble as rubble
in the blue Empire.

I've left everything behind, for an endpaper shore; to lie under
membranous layers, as lights
vault, coagulate, rebound –

To see one ignite another, billowing, and genealogies decline;
to watch here day's ardour
that turns water into wine.

Other People

There are rain-pebbles, late,
across black windows, streetlight on them;
they hang like conglomerate
in the cement walls of a mausoleum,

which is the darkness. Or it's steel, fused
as if a lever were thrown
when cars pass. Clear dark is bruised
where a figure sits. The phone

keeps on. Headlights splash as though
trying to wash from the wall
a realization. One that won't let go
for anyone who'd call.

—

A public phone and pine trees on
the edge of the paddocks. You see a man
cross an oily concrete apron
to the shop's bowser. A crushed beer can

in here, a cigarette's long ash
on the ledge. The directory says, 'My Fault,'
underscored. 'Come on Babe.' Your cash
dangles. Echo-sounds a black vault.

The cow's rump is a rowboat that takes
a wave-crest. Gritty miniatures –
a camphor laurel's lime then silver flakes;
a cloud like steam, claws over claws.

Sixteen Poems from the Japanese

Even now, I never linger
by this valley stream,
in case my shadow
flows back into the world.
       – Dōgen

Ah, how many dewdrops are falling
from the stems of grass,
now that the autumn winds have come
to the fields of Miyagino?
       – Saigyo

Sorcerer, who flies through heaven,
find for me the one
who has never yet appeared,
not even in my dreams.
    — Murasaki

In the shade of a willow
by the road
the clear water is running.
I meant to pause here
only a moment.
    — Saigyo

Water drips from moss
among the mountain stones,
and I am rendered clear.
    — Ryokan

The days that have gone by
leave one sad,
and yet they were all of them
only a dream.
    — Former Emperor Hanazono

I sit and look back on
days that have gone.
Did I dream them all,
am I dreaming now?
Listening to winter rain.
    — Ryokan

A light snowfall
and within that
a billion worlds arise
and within that
a light snowfall.
    — Ryokan

Haze rises
at the end of a spring day
that I have spent with children
bouncing ball.
      – Ryokan

As the sunset ends
and the mountains are hidden,
further off
other mountains appear.
      – Kyoguku Tamekame

In my home town
the cherries are in bloom
and spring is passing by
the same as ever.
      – Dōgen

Early summer rain
has left in the roadway
a hall of light.
      – Basho

Ah, look!
The mushroom-gatherers missed
five dewdrops.
      – Buson

A camellia fell;
the monk smiled
going by.
      – Hori Bakusui

Clear autumn day;
my wife doesn't even notice
we pass each other.
      – Nishigaki Shu

> The crows' calling
> ends.
> Twilight snow.
>   – Aro Usuda

Translated with Kazuaki Tanahashi; Zen Centre, San Francisco, 1982

The Shark

Those inconceivable acres of the sea's looseness are made to jostle
and shimmy;
it is an immense, light-tainted
thin jelly.

The sea is shouldering and displacing itself about itself
on the roused and dissembling plain,
harried like migrant reindeer,
lava-bright or wind-torn.

The diver keeps on steadily sinking from there, spread on shadow
as to drown;
weighted, he feels ducked and
pole-pressured down;

only his breath seems to panic, and he turns to watch it pass,
wobbling and clinking upwards
into light,
a stairwell the mind climbs on and breaks like glass.

The long sunlight sways here
in columns, as though a bundle of lift cables.
With its withered Red Indian head
a turtle's

struggling up steeply
on stumpy wings – an ennui, bound in horn,
a broken beak.
Bevies of fish are making little mouths to squeak

like society girls, in their spotted or banded
wafting chiffon,
and with impenetrable dead eyes. The jelly fish
are big parcels of frog spawn.

Something stares sideways,
that has a worn-down Caligula profile; its teeth like a fender.
And as a spinning hoop,
when it is coming to rest, surrounds a

centre, with touches of all parts of the rim,
so in leathern skirt the rat-tailed
manta ray, flapping,
is hung in the grit it's flailed.

The shark comes drifting with silent engine
through water thick as smoke,
a space craft that is called on by a distant gravity
out of the murk;

but it can loosely swathe
its limber grey fuselage.
It moves with all the potential and ease of someone
turning out of a garage.

The long body wavers beautifully
and easily,
as a train at dusk
through the curves on the floor of a valley.

The gills, for all their frightful deepness,
are each neat
as a Japanese slit;
the head's simply rounded-off and incorporate

like the nose of a surfboard – it is not the authority
for anything within;
the head, amid jungle light, seems less important
than its fin.

It has the senile, yellow, ill-wishing look
of a hillbilly grandma's
uncomprehending eyes, and what seems her mouth
in its Greek mask melancholy or tooth-stump uncouth.

But a foolish guffaw,
and that vacuousness is filled with a double barbed wire;
or, closer,
a wreath, and each leaf a razor.

The mouth is a picketing of backward serrations;
the skin, sliding ground glass.
The diver waits with his single fang poised, for the tonnage
of its flick-pass –

imagining the voluptuous greedy wriggle
of its packed dog's body
and himself clamped too overwhelmingly, too rigid,
for struggle.

This energy, this pure appetite, that's below
and before the mind, this
is the thriving pathology
which is life; here elegant, as though wriggled from a thesis.

Weakened and divided in us, this still has to be allowed for,
it is basic;
in me it has a voice,
each has a shark.

And what shall we do with this?
All things are unstable and flowing, as if the modes of one thing:
is it possible this could modify?
It would have to be shaped through knowing.

Only through understanding,
by staying watchful and still.
The effort to change is, as with art, love, religion, a deviousness
of the shark-like will.

Morality we learned
from being outdone in immorality. Ultimately, from Zeus.
By wanting some time
for something other than oneself. Morality is a truce.

It arises from whence
so much evil sets forth – out of boredom. But is knowledge
and strength. It's to face our nature, without wanting to disclaim,
and to call that by its name.

Description of a Walk

In the shape of long sand-dunes, but apple green,
the pastures that I'd crossed. A quivering rain
hung above them. One currawong somewhere, warbling
happily as a hose within a drain.

The forest was cumulus on stilts, from afar;
everywhere within it, leaf-splatterings and spar;
the leaves, paint clots, or a fringe of trickling.
Angry as a burned insect, a distant car.

The forest closed. I climbed amongst sandstone –
great gouts of lava, petrified as iron;
puffed like fungi, or with a broken iceberg's edge;
all of a rusty red or burnt orange tone.

About the plinths and mantels was an artful
pebble-scatter; on its pedestal, an eccentric bowl.
Rose-coloured sandstone syncopated salt.
Blowing rain was being emptied by the bushel.

Uphill, warped arcades of bush, rack on rack;
reiterative as cuneiforms. Bacon redness of bark,
or smooth wet trunks of caterpillar green,
and some with a close dog's fur, greyish black.

Other colours: Brazil nut kernel, an unfired pit.
In the wet, tart as bush smoke, a sweet rot.
The air rain-threaded, as though with insect sounds.
My heart flapped like a lizard's, by the top.

Underneath a clay bank, an old grey gutter,
now sealed with rare smoked glass. A claw of water
flexed nearby, on rock ledges, and over roots –
its wide-toothed, vibrating cane-rake clatter.

Sprigged trees, and vista of Pre-Raphaelite shine:
beneath gentian hills, a billiard table green;
ploughed land, pumpernickel; the road, a fracture;
the shapes of coral in a dark tree-line.

Rain shaded to silence. To cicadas' shekel
sound. – Emptied from a bucket, a pile of shell
poured with the numerous headlong pour of sand
onto other shells. A dry calcite rattle.

And this merely the start – warming of an engine.
Each opens a row of gills; if you find one
you see almost through the body. Their joined hums'
tremendous power, an electricity substation.

I walked on and on, in such vibrance. Wet light
gave the leaves' undersides a stainless glint.
Rag and bone bushland. White arms lifted, dangling
cloth. That chant. What it was all about I forgot.

A Winter Morning

For a few minutes more now, all the day's furniture
will remain sheeted, in a shuttered room.
With their glow of sucked-thin barley sugar
the lights way off at the by-pass are still drooping in bloom.
Here, only two headlights, on a lane,
easing downstairs. In wood and fibro, my cathedral town –
such this valley. *Materia* is *mater*; substance is womb.

I go along backyard fences through some fog –
most are patched with old corrugated iron –
onto a plumed, translating hillslope, with someone's dog;
the sky is lifting, become woodgrain:
all the dabs, whirls, darts, long streaks of golden cloud
on cloud. The weeds wear strung fruit, or a globed
insect's opal glitter. I skirt the dank tree-line....

Those eucalyptus, the blue of solemn voices.
Elevated, descending, they've all of them graves and accents
flying. I'm here on a Sunday, for the offices
of matter – poinsettias, more red than sacraments;
a sceptred palm tree's golden smoulder; the insouciance
of levitated cerulean; the grass's effulgence....
It is the same lesson: ease of their relinquishments.

A Summer Evening

They still do as was always done:
they call the children just on night
then make sure of the fly-screen catch,
while moths knock down a shaggy pinch
off themselves or the porch light.

And insects race their bobbins, thick
as a sweat shop, as grass itch,
as matted grass seeds that get stuck
smudgily in bleached leg-hairs.
Another sound: a nutmeg-grater scratch.

It is the time of 'Look at yourselves!'
One who's not a parent gazes out
at tree-shapes spread like peacocks on
a lake (the town); at grass-loop shine;
at the empty lit set-up of this street.

And likes the way a paling fence below
is reclining into weeds. A thickened tree
by the house has its bole brush-swiped
with shadow. At this time the milkman came.
Now, the marching-girl flickers of TV.

A horse crops close around arc-lights'
twin metal poles, in the paddock next door,
that rise from concrete for a car-yard
and make a light of grainy plastic there.
A snapshot from a passing car.

Another way, the neon signs, and trees
ragged as weeds; and the last, squeezed light,
beautiful and calm – as when illness emptied
her face. And you had thought, Why not
like this always? Why now, too late?

Nine Bowls of Water

Clear water, in silvery tin dishes
dented as ping pong balls:
a lemon juice tinge of the staling light is in them;
they've a faint lid of dust.

A potted water along a board slopped
and dripping lightly.
While the men work on the city road, excavating
its charred blackness,

the water waits
behind a corrugated iron shed that is set
at the pavement front,
under the tall shadowing empty stadium.

On that low plank, also, crude soap pieces,
bright as the fat
of gutted chickens – but, with a closer look, resistant,
darkly-cracked, like old bone handles –

one beside each bowl,
and the rags are on their bits of hooked wire.
The cars continue,
but few people walk here between the lunch shed

and brick wall. Set out along a wet bench,
the kneeling water:
this reality from which we have dreamed the spirit.
We walk in grittiness,

on papers, mud-scrapings,
splattered with a sporadic jackhammer racket,
past nine bowls of water – a gallantry of the union.
Trees in avenues and sailing boats and women.

put brochure
14 Captain Row